"Some say goalkeepers are crazy. Anyone who has spent time between the sticks and doesn't have this book certainly is crazy. It's a must have."
– Bob Wilson in The Comet/The Gooner

"The perfect stocking filler for anyone who has ever taken their place between the sticks or simply goes wobbly at the knees at the mere mention of Uhlsport, Sondico or Coffer. Exclusive interviews and anecdotes from some of the game's goalkeeping greats. Lavishly designed. Stunning. Magnificent." **– TheSportsman.com**

"The attention to detail is stunning. Memories jump off the page; you can almost smell the PU from a pair of Sondico Pro File. Stokes' love for all things goalkeeping really comes across in his writing. The layout is a feast for the eyes. An ideal stocking filler for the goalkeeper in your life. Excellent." **– The Football Pink**

"A great present from the grandchildren."
– Tony Coton

"An absolute must for any goalkeeping nut. Top job, Rob!"
– Adam Sells

Conker Editions Ltd
22 Cosby Road
Littlethorpe
Leicester
LE19 2HF
Email: books@conkereditions.co.uk
Website: www.conkereditions.co.uk
First published by Conker Editions Ltd 2020
A CIP catalogue record for this book is available from the British Library.
13-digit ISBN: 9781999900861
Design and typesetting by Gary Silke.
Printed in the UK by Mixam.

GLOVE STORY 2

Another book for every goalkeeper, past and present

Rob Stokes, Derek Hammond & Gary Silke

with illustrations by Doug Nash

CONKER

special days for seriously ill young adults

FOREWORD by BobWilson

Glove Story 2 is here. Sequels can be a serious challenge and often never live up to the original; but this second, companion volume of goalkeeping memories and memorabilia even surpasses the joy we all found in *Glove Story* when Rob, Derek and Gary brought flooding back the trials and tribulations of playing in the most challenging position within a football team.

Once again we are vividly transported back in time to when we goalkeepers became heroes for an hour or a day, enjoying the plaudits of a match-winning save; when we playfully sought to recreate the heroics of Banks's miracle save against Pele, or even dared to compare our own

Seaman's claw back from Sheffield United's Paul Peschisolido in the 2003 FA Cup semi.

We all can recall the greatest saves we've ever witnessed or made. We keepers live off such memories when trusting our instinct and honed skills in defying the odds. And

just as clearly we remember the times when our decision-making occasionally failed us and made us look vulnerable, crazy enough to try and fill a goal measuring eight yards by eight feet. That's 192 square feet. A massive, bloody great chasm.

The memories keep popping into my mind when watching today's game and seeing the keepers' latest equipment – expensive, personally tailored gloves that would look appropriate for Neil Armstrong and those men who walked on the moon.

Back in the year dot, in my era, we depended on our bare hands, aided maybe by a chewing gum spit to make the fingers sticky and tacky. The alternative in the '60s for a decade were the green 'gardening gloves' that bore the name of Gordon Banks or Peter Bonetti. They cost about five shillings;

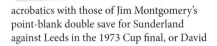

acrobatics with those of Jim Montgomery's point-blank double save for Sunderland against Leeds in the 1973 Cup final, or David

incredible value compared to the cost of the thick, rubber-faced gloves worn by every top keeper today. And how do they compare? On a dry day back then, nothing could beat bare hands and spit. The green cotton gloves

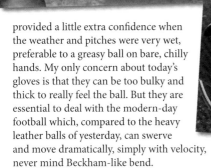

During my career I suffered broken fingers and wrist, several broken ribs, a punctured lung, dislocated elbow, torn knee ligaments and cartilage and numerous cuts to the head. But my advice to any aspiring keeper has always been the same – trust your instincts. My crazy saves became my trademark. We can't all be fortunate enough to have the cool, calm presence of a Pat Jennings or David Seaman. If it works for you, go for it. The bulk of goalkeeping skills are predictable. The 'daring' can help make the difference between a save and a goal, between a 'good' game and 'great' game.

So, here we go again – *Glove Story 2*, sharing our obsession with memories, heroes, dreams

provided a little extra confidence when the weather and pitches were very wet, preferable to a greasy ball on bare, chilly hands. My only concern about today's gloves is that they can be too bulky and thick to really feel the ball. But they are essential to deal with the modern-day football which, compared to the heavy leather balls of yesterday, can swerve and move dramatically, simply with velocity, never mind Beckham-like bend.

Happily, one thing that will never change is the impact a 'hero' can make upon you. As a kid growing up in Chesterfield, I would stand behind the goal of Ron Powell or a very young Gordon Banks. Both were athletic and gymnastic in style, and I learned from them.

However, my real hero was Bert Trautmann, the former German POW who played on with a broken neck in the 1956 FA Cup final. The Trautmann head-first saves came as second nature to me, the thrilling elements of surprise and speed often saving a goal, and the day for the team. You could pay a heavy price for this uncompromising style.

and with each other. The authors transport us back once more to our second homes, under the bar, between the sticks, patrolling the 18-yard box, eyeing up that 12-yard penalty spot and assessing the variety of playing surfaces from pristine pitches to mud heaps.

The history is all here, and so too is the present-day role. Read it, enjoy it, smile and maybe shed a tear. *Glove Story 2* recreates the unique feeling of our chosen position on a football field, unlike any other when it comes to individuality and courage.

Those two vital characteristics will never change for all of us who are obsessed by the crazy world that is goalkeeping.

INTRODUCTION

"I'm a born-again collector. I collected avidly as a boy, and then I stopped. But then, equally mysteriously, it all came flooding back – the joys and delights and agonies of collecting… Oh, if only I still had all those little, stupid, piddling scruffy things I collected as a boy, none of them valuable, even now, but so full of memories and emotions." – Hunter Davies, *Confessions of a Collector*

cool clobber from brands such as Uhlsport, Reusch and Sondico Sports.

Paulsgrove keeper Mark Cannell stood out from all the rest for just one reason. His fantastic gloves and kit. He was the first I ever saw decked out head to toe in Uhlsport gear – and, to this day, he likes to remind me regularly that he was the first in Portsmouth to wear a silver shadow Uhlsport jersey and 036 gloves.

Mark got to know my dad due to his table-topping side's match reports, and rang the doorbell one night to give me a Uhlsport catalogue, realising I was on the crazy pathway of wanting to be a goalkeeper. Along with the Sukan Sports catalogues popping through the letterbox every August, this marked the start of my collecting obsession.

However, by the end of the '90s I'd stopped playing and had moved to London. And that's when my dad rang to ask what I wanted him to do with the two bags in the garage that were full of gloves and glovebags. For the last few seasons I'd started to keep all the pairs I'd worn, irrespective of condition and the smell of them, so there was a fair few in those bags. But I was short of space in my new place and my love for playing football had disappeared.

The clue's in the tracksuit bottoms, gloves and glovebag…

For any keeper, old gloves are associated with countless memories and emotions – from your first pair of basic green cottons to the first proper pair that promised to put you on a par with the pros, hanging there on the sports shop rack.

Back in the late '70s my dad worked part time as a roving reporter on Saturday afternoons, covering Portsmouth parks football for the *Sports Mail*. He'd frantically fill his notebooks, ready to phone in his copy at half-time to catch the deadline for the 6pm edition. Meanwhile, me and my brother kicked around in the back of the nets. And, thanks mostly to his wayward shooting rather than my expert tipping over the bar, there was a near-constant plea of "Can we have our ball back, Keeps?" Even then, I was already eyeing up the keepers'

THE ULTIMATE GLOVE!!

021 by Uhlsport

In sizes 8, 9, &10
Available now!!

"Chuck them in the bin," I replied. "I've got no use for them." Ouch! That still hurts, even today. Inside those bags were about five pairs

8

of matchworn Uhlsports and a glovebag from Bryan Gunn.

So, what got me back into collecting? Initially, I spotted a pair of gloves listed on

know I was always looking to find the old gloves from the past, and messaged me one evening on my commuter train out of London. He'd popped into his local sports shop and asked the lovely ladies, who had run the place since the '60s, if they had any old gloves in their stockroom. A steady stream of 23 photos followed – each one of

Didi and Gigi, and Rob's long-lost Marmite specials.

eBay by Dave Holmes, the former owner of Sukan Sports. They were part of the old stock he'd kept after the shop had closed down. However these weren't just any old pair of gloves, these were a pair of Uhlsport 023s, still in their original box. The first pair of proper gloves I ever had. After snapping these up, it took me on a quest to try and get all the pairs I'd once worn – and then all the gloves I'd ever yearned for but had been unable to afford, with the aim of trying to preserve the history of the goalkeeping glove for many years to come.

One pair that had eluded me for ages was the Uhlsport 021 – a 'Marmite' glove due to the thickness of the palm and the hard wrist-strap that required tape to keep it firmly secured. Plus its 'iconic' status as the pair worn by Peter Shilton at Mexico '86.

Enter Christian Parlee of Toronto, Canada. A shirt collector of good stock, he'd got to

brand new, boxed gloves, including a pair of 021s sparkling like diamonds in a pile of coal. I've never been able to thank Christian, or Didi and Gigi, enough.

And so to the latest chapter in my *Glove Story*, and the involvement of Bob Wilson, which has led not only to some wonderful, original content but also the chance to meet a hero I'd only previously considered in terms of football cards, goalkeeping schools and cherished TV clips. Thanks to Bob for all his kindness, help and input.

All in all, I hope you find the *Glove Story* books, and the long goalkeeping journey they illuminate, a good advert for becoming an obsessive collector of sometimes less than fragrant chunks of ancient latex!

WHAT A CARD

To kick things off with a powerful punt into unfamiliar territory, here's a selection of football cards that gives a rare flavour of goalkeeping culture from bygone ages and exotic climes.

The fashions and methods may at first seem strange, but we hope you share our warm feeling of timeless kinship with these keepers, all instantly recognisable as devoted to our common, obsessive aim. Stopping the ball from hitting the back of the net.

At any cost.

No matter whether they hail from the Cold War era, from inter-war Spain or Edwardian England, there's no mistaking these distant relatives' lifetime membership of the good old Goalkeepers' Union.

As we were looking for a glimpse back in time beyond the nostalgic glow of the common football cards and stickers of our youth – back to the age of the giant flat cap and even the loose rope crossbar – we enlisted the help of the ultimate football card collector. You're in safe hands. Our old friend Carl Wilkes is author of the *A-to-Z of Football Collectibles: Priceless Cigarette Cards and Sought-After Soccer Stickers.*

Going back to the very earliest days of the football card, Carl's first selection was the four different Baines issues dating between 1900 and 1920. So-called 'Baines shields' featured a huge number of football teams and players in their club colours, first sold as early as 1885. Kids bought packets of the cards for a ha'penny each, flicked and swapped to their hearts' content, and then had the option to send in their cards for the chance to win a football jersey – hence the rarity value of the cards, to this day.

Fulham, Accrington and Clifton Trinity goalkeepers are

Football - Thépot

Early Baines football cards can now be worth between £100 and £1,000. But watch this space...

SÉRIE DE 136 IMAGES

I N D I A N A

41. HIDEN SAUTE
DEVANT COURTOIS

Si le *Football-Club* de Sochaux a échoué dans la Coupe de France, il vient de terminer brillamment le championnat de France professionnel. Il est vrai qu'il dispose des services de brillants joueurs, et notamment de Courtois. On voit sur le cliché le goal parisien Hiden prévenant tant bien que mal un shoot de Courtois « en chemise brune ».

C'est un produit "DONAT"
Fabriqué en France par
Mon JEAN - DONAT DUPONT LILLE

41 Hiden saute devant Courtois

featured on three of the Baines cards, while the other round issue plays cruelly on the 'goalkeeper's nightmare': the Bradford company dips into old Yorkshire dialect to chide the would-be shotstopper for being 'afraid of the ball'.

While we were grateful to Carl for his pick of the best goalie cards of all time, what we secretly wanted to know was which was the rarest. You know, just in case we happened to spot one at a car boot sale. And, of course, while it's the art and the history that's

important, we may as well find out about the value, too...

"The Jorda Chocolate card of Girona's Josep Prats is one of the rarest of the cards," Carl told us, "but the Dutch transfer of the Russian goalie from the 1952

Olympic Games is the one! That is a diamond in rarity stakes. It's one heck of a rare card, even rarer than the Baines cards."

So now you know. But don't bother checking on eBay, because we just beat you to the last one, up for 99p, Buy It Now!

Just for the record, Josep Prats was a legendary goalie for the Spanish side Unió Deportiva Girona between 1922 and 1930. If you have a copy of the original *Glove Story* on your bookshelf, you may recognise the curious kneeguards and the trendy white knitted jersey from our story of the amazing Barcelona goalie, Ricardo Zamora. We said then that we wanted to know more about the mysterious puppet Zamora was posing with between the sticks, and now we know it must have been a fashion

Ivanov   Rusland

FUTBOL
CAMPEONATOS NACIONALES

1958
PRIMERA DIVISIÓN
030
REPRODUCCIONES A TODO COLOR.

World Cup 1966

BANKS, Engeland

Cup Jules Rimet

Behende wie ein Fisch im Wasser

GARTMANN SCHOKOLADE   Serie 635, Bild 5

CCCP

LEV YASHIN · RUSIA

Wim Landman : Voetballen

BERT TRAUTMANN, MANCHESTER CITY

SERIES of 40 NO.21

GOALKEEPER

205.- Ron Springett
Arquero al estilo sudame-
ricano.

100 YARDS
Amateur
Champio
PLAY UP
DARLINGTON
WHARTON.

for Spanish goalies between the wars. Possibly a goalies' take on voodoo to scare off opposition attackers.

On these spreads, football trade cards from Germany and France are shown alongside those of Spain and the UK, issues that were designed to attract more sales of a particular brand or retailer's wares, whether chocolate, chicory or tea.

On the fascinating subject of rare cards' value as an investment, Carl told us: "The Baines cards are priceless in a sense: if you sell them, you'll probably never get them again, and no insurance money could buy them back if they were ever purloined or destroyed.

"That said, most Baines cards range from just into triple figures going on into four figures. There exists a handful of each, at the most; but mostly there's only one or two copies of each."

That's the case with the 1885 Baines card of legendary sprinter and Darlington goalkeeper Arthur Wharton; but this one is different. It was probably the first football card ever printed.

"Very rare cards are currently enjoying a period of almost exponential growth," Carl says, "but I believe they are due a further leap in value. There are 1,000 Mickey Mantle 1952 gum cards believed to exist, but one has already sold for $3 million! There are over 50 Honus Wagner baseball cigarette cards, from 1909, believed to exist; but two have sold for over $3 million each...

"Wharton? Only one or two Wharton Baines cards are known to exist. Different cards, each of them. Mine is one of one, as far as I know.

Soccer is growing faster than any other sport as a world collectible. Americans are moving into it big time. Wharton will be the first million-pound soccer card, and hopefully sooner rather than later."

NOT SO SUPER-STITIONS

Talking to so many great old keepers over the past couple of years, one recurrent topic has turned up unbidden in countless conversations. It's spooky how much time and effort us goalies pour into bizarre superstitions – always so much more reliable than the traditional alternative of long days on the training ground!

David Seaman set the ball rolling with a personal tale of an everyday OCD tic: "I always had to be number two coming out behind the captain," he admitted – only to be trumped by a succession of ex-cats. Joe Corrigan and his sprig of heather. Eddie Niedzwiecki touching the wall above the dressing-room door. Fabien Barthez and his lucky kissable bonce.

But we can do better than that, can't we, keepers?

Mark Crossley definitely had a strange gleam in his eye when he told us enthusiastically: "I went through a spell at Forest of putting my left shin pad

LUCKY FOR JOE

Before every home match, Manchester City keeper Joe Corrigan gets a sprig of white heather. It's a good luck gesture from flower seller Helen Turner.

Judging by Joe's consistent displays over the years, that heather must be powerful stuff.

on first, then I would go to the shower room and throw a ball at the wall, always catching it in sequences of four".

But that was nothing compared to Bryan

'KEEPER'S AMAZIN MATCH-DAY RITUAL

Gunn's somewhat more worrying confession: "Something that started when I was at Aberdeen. I would always come out and attempt to head the crossbar – much to the amusement of the home supporters. Sir Alex Ferguson and Archie Knox would always say my other ritual was picking my knickers out my bum!"

Back in the '90s, Oldham's Jon Hallworth went four better, listing his obsessive checklist of superstitions in *Match* magazine: left boot first, left glove first, shake hands with all team-mates, score during the kickaround… and no haircut before the match!

But there's no doubt which goalie takes the all-time biscuit when it comes to bucketfuls of not-so-superstitions. Partick Thistle's Alan Rough opened up to the *Topical Times Football Book* about his various lucky talismans – old tennis ball, lucky keyring, star-shaped medal, miniature football boot he once found in the back of his net – and that was just for starters. In the dressing room, Alan always headed for peg number 13 and wore an old Partick number 11 jersey under his own shirt. Next came the three bounces of a ball on the tunnel wall, the blast into the empty net… and not forgetting the cap full of hankies.

That's right. Roughie's ultimate superstition was to blow his nose as many times as possible throughout the course of the match, keeping his stock of snot-rags stored snugly next to his lucky perm.

Taking the Rough with the smooth: Alan relied on lucky charms to try and keep a clean sheet.

13

PAUL TREVILLION GLOVES – DESIGNED FOR PAT JENNINGS

In Hunter Davies's *The Glory Game*, there's a tantalising reference to gloves designed in the early '70s by *Roy of the Rovers* artist/Beaver Sports supremo Paul Trevillion. So we asked Paul about the gloves – and he only went and sent us his drawing of the prototypes!

"Pat wasn't impressed," Paul laughed. "He said it made his hands look even larger. Pat was not too enamoured by the media who used to call his hands 'shovels'. A *Sunday People* article mentioned that Pat could hold four oranges in one hand!

PLAYING KIT

GARY SPRAKE

Leeds United goalkeeper Gary Sprake always puts a little mud on his gloves when playing in wet weather. This is a wise precaution and one well worth copying for it acts just like an adhesion and helps the wet ball stick instead of slipping through your grasp.

the glove, like Velcro.

"The prototype gloves were originally for Gary Sprake but unfortunately the Liverpool nickname 'Careless Hands' meant I was forced to switch to Pat Jennings."

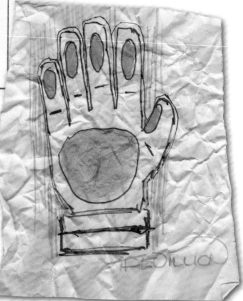

"Today the glove would be a multi-million seller, and goalkeepers would stop dropping the ball or palming it away. As in the '60s and '70s, they would go back to catching it cleanly as all goalkeepers did before those big MICKEY MOUSE gloves came into fashion. The Trevillion glove enabled TOUCH AND FEEL!

"The finger and palm cut-outs gave that secure, natural hand feel. In wet weather the cut-outs were a different material to

14

AND A HAPPY BESPOKE BIRTHDAY TO YOU

Whether you were a goalie during your schooldays or one of those other, lesser footballers who runs around all over the pitch, you'll remember that special sinking feeling that was reserved for birthday and Christmas Day mornings.

The source of our shared collective pain was the generic football card. Your mum and all your aunties knew you were a football nut, so they got you a special footy birthday card with 'Now You Are 9' embossed over Leicester City's non-existent yellow shirts and Bruce Grobbelaar's fall from grace, there was the added bottom-clenching embarr-

Have a Great Birthday, HUSBAND!

a five-year-old action shot of an entirely random, incidental match – or one of those gruesome artist watercolours with made-up kit. The purples vs. the yellow and blue hoops.

Of course, it was tougher for Nanny and for you if you happened to be a goalie. It isn't easy, finding a birthday card with a keeper on it, so apart from having to keep quiet about assment that you weren't really all that much of a Manchester United fan, and that goalies had been wearing gloves for the past ten years or so.

Now, give your Auntie Kath a big kiss and say 'thank you', and *don't be so ungrateful.*

15

NUMBER ONE

What a privilege to gaze upon some of the superb black-and-white portraits from Robert Wilson's *One* – a timeless and very special goalkeeping book. And not only did Robert give us permission to reproduce some of our favourite shots, he also agreed to a chat to give us some insight into its creation.

So, how did the idea come about, and how long did it take to pin down all these keepers to be photographed?

"The idea came about as I was assisting other photographers at the time, but wanted a project I could shoot myself to give me practice and hone my techniques. I had one light, one canvas background that I'd painted myself, and limited film and equipment. I was inspired by a set of portraits by one of my favourite photographers, Albert Watson. He'd shot a series of portraits of prisoners within the American prisons. I loved his black-and-white images and liked the feeling of individuality and isolation. My natural thought went to goalkeepers, having been a keeper myself. And, having the opportunity of using my dad's connections, it was a way of bringing two loves together."

Was it a case of travelling round all the clubs and capturing them after they'd finished training? (It's only Kevin Pressman who seems to be in his back garden!) That must have taken some serious organisation?

"Yes, I'd have to get in touch through Dad, and set up a time that was convenient. I travelled all round the country in my old Toyota Corolla with the background barely fitting in. Most were shot at the training ground...

and, as you recognised, Kevin Pressman was at his home! The whole thing took nearly a year to complete. You'll notice from the contact sheets, they were all printed by myself in my small home darkroom to keep costs down. That's why they all look a bit of a mess. Also, you'll see the holes in the contact sheets where I cut out the images I was going to use when we were putting the book order together."

What was the feedback from the keepers when the book came out? Did they have a say in the photos you used?

"No, no one had a say in what images were used. All just trusted me. In those days there really wasn't as much paranoia and marketing around the players. It would be a much harder project to do just based on trust today. It would have to go through many layers of red tape, I'm sure, and then those involved would all want guarantees for 'what's in it for them'. This was a time when all the players just saw that it was a project being shot because of a love for the position. Occasionally, one of the keepers would make a comment about the image – Bruce Grobbelaar, for instance. I had him looking at me in the goal, through the net,

With a bullet: Robert's book of keeper portraits was a sure-fire bestseller.

and he commented: 'I get it, Robert... caught in the net'. This wasn't long after his court case about match fixing. But the keepers themselves seem to love the images. I think it was just nice for them all to get a book that just highlighted their unique position on a football field."

I noticed that only five keepers (including your dad) wore gloves in the photos. Did you consciously want to focus more on the hands than on our tools of the trade?

"No, that wasn't intentional; although, whenever I've shot football players I've seemed to strip them down to their own attributes. I shot Dennis Bergkamp once and made him take his boots off, so I could get a shot of his bare feet. To me, a pair of boots or gloves are just objects that could be made by anyone, whereas the hands or the feet of the person are actually the heroic elements."

One photo that really stood out for me was the one of Keith Branagan's battle-worn knees. Did you have a particular favourite?

"Well, obviously, I've always loved the David Seaman cover image. You'll notice from the contact sheet, the image only came about after I cropped the original frame quite heavily so that it only showed one hand instead of both. There are plenty of other shots that I love due to either having a great subject or the fact that what I was trying technically came off; but one of

my favourite images has always been the one of Neville Southall. I loved everything about that image. The way the light only just catches his eyes, the strength of contrast in the image, how hard he looks and of course how prominent and white the number 1 stood out on his jersey."

Finally, do you have any plans to do an updated version for the Premier era?

"Well, as we said, these things are much harder to put together these days with sponsors, agents, managers all having a say. It would need to be a much bigger project with a common goal in mind. You never know, though..."

Chatting to Pat Jennings about his playing days, and very early into our conversation I found out we had one important thing in common. Pat's favourite glove was the Uhlsport 034, which he famously wore at two World Cup finals. I'd love to say that we also had similar styles in goalkeeping, but as Bob Wilson was happy to admit: "I couldn't coach Pat. He was a one-off, often unorthodox. What could I teach him? Jennings was the most naturally gifted goalkeeper I ever set eyes on."

When I was a young lad, I wrote to my goalkeeping hero asking for his autograph, and within a few days came a reply from Highbury. I still have the photo to this day...

Given that the Trevillion Pat Jennings gloves never came to fruition, were there any other offers from glove companies?

"No, I never had any glove companies wanting to put my name to their products other than Paul. I had a good relationship with Uhlsport, who would supply me with free gloves, but I never signed a paid contract as I really didn't want to be tied down to one company. However, I may as well have done, given the amount of years I wore them for. Before wearing Uhlsport, I did sign an agreement for balls, sports bags and football

boots with my signature on and a PJ logo; but they never did gloves for some reason."

Did you just say there were PJ boots?

"Yes, I still got some, too. After this call I'll dig them out and send you a photo! When I was at Tottenham I was approached by Hummel to endorse the same white pair that Alan Ball was wearing, which would have made me the first goalkeeper to wear them."

I've never seen any footage or adverts with you wearing them?

"You wouldn't, because the first time I turned up at training with them on, Bill Nicholson spotted them. He politely told me that I wouldn't be wearing them, to get them off my feet and get back in your black pair. So that was the end of that!"

Turning to gloves...

In the 1978 FA Cup final you wore the basic green cotton gloves. But by the following season you'd been introduced to the Adidas Curkovic gloves…

"Thinking back now, these would have come from the Adidas rep. At that time I was wearing their boots, so I'm sure he would

PAT JENNINGS
AT
Argos

Top class goalie dressed as a Unipart filter has large lumps of dark, oily masses hurled towards him.

He makes brilliant save after save.
Commentator: "An oil filter is like a goalkeeper."

that I wore, so each time I dived and made a save, they then had to hose it down and wipe it clean each time after every take!"

You never took up the great '80s fashion and used a Uhlsport glovebag, but instead just opted for a silver carrier bag...

"There wasn't any particularly reason for it. I wasn't really fussed, to be honest. I just needed something to keep a spare pair of gloves in along with a cap, chewing gum, plus some spare tie-ups.

have given me them to try out. They were certainly an upgrade from the cotton pairs, and did take a while to get used to."

Did you ever have gloves specially made for you, as has been claimed?

"No, nor did they come and take moulds of my hands. I just wore gloves straight out of the box which they sent me. Normally size 9.5, as I liked to wear them tight fitting."

You wore the 034 model in two successive World Cups, and helped to make them truly iconic. And the same with other products, too: Cookstown sausages, Ariel washing powder, Frosties with Tony the Tiger!

"You got me thinking now. There was also an advert I did for NatWest Bank which carried the slogan 'Saving without Struggle'. They'd made this extendable arm which would reach out and save the ball whilst I was reading a newspaper. Also, they had me sitting on the crossbar saving the ball with my feet. With the Unipart advert, the producer of the commercial didn't realise that goalmouths got quite muddy. They'd only made one of the filters

Commentator: "A Unipart filter will save your engine from..."

Commentator: "...grime...dirt ...and pollution..."

I also used to keep a little prayer in there, too, which my mother sent me along with a medal of St Jude."

MY GOALKEEPING HERO

Bryan Gunn | Ray Clemence

"A brilliant, classy goalkeeper who I saw live at Pittodrie in a European Cup tie. Even better was seeing him play in the Ronnie Corbett golf classic at Royal Aberdeen, where he played a shot out of a burn in his bare feet! A true goalkeeping great who is now a golfing friend of mine."

TOTTENHAM HOTSPUR

PAT JENNINGS
GOALKEEPER

19

THE EARLY YEARS

When you look back at how glove technology has evolved over the years, you do have to wonder how the keepers of our nostalgic Golden

Four strips of ping-pong bat material for punching power!

Era ever managed to catch or even hold a ball with such apparent ease.

Whether you were playing on a rain-soaked pitch or a mudbath, heavy leather match balls became deadly projectiles seemingly designed to damage goalkeepers' hands and fingers.

Keepers had no choice but to take a fair selection of gloves out on to the pitch, just to make sure they could get through the match, fighting an eternal battle against them becoming waterlogged or clogged up with mud or sand.

Every goalie was forced to become a quick-change artist in order to stem the tide – provided, of course, they were lucky enough to have spare

pairs of gloves available in their glovebag.

The glove change was a special skill that needed total focus, keeping one eye on the field of play as you chose your moment to dash back into your net, fumble for a new pair and make the switch before the oppo loomed within shooting distance.

Many a time, you'd be making saves with only one glove on after you'd been caught short.

Many experiments were made to discover the best type of grip that could be delivered, ranging from your standard school-playground glove with

strips of table-tennis bat material stuck to the fingers, through to those produced by Gola and Mikasa, with small black pimples

20

and velvet hogskin to nappa or velvet leather and polyurethane, while palms were fashioned from smooth foam rubber, neoprene, dimpled napping or waffled cotton interlock!

extruding from the palms – similar to those that can be found today on the shelves of B&Q and various builders' merchants.

Looking back at the patents and packaging for the early gloves, the exotic materials used could run from stretch nylon, sueded peccary

From a collecting point of view, I love it when early gloves are still in their original cardboard boxes, as it reminds me of the days of entering Drayton Sports, where they would have the range of Peter Bonetti and Phil Parkes Metric gloves proudly dangling from their counter display stand.

KEEPERS & THEIR SPONSORED MOTORS

It's a nice little perk of the job, isn't it? A mid-range executive saloon provided by one of the club's sponsors, or even a glove

manufacturer. And who's a humble goalie to complain if the price to pay is your name stencilled over the driver's door in six-inch letters?

If it was good enough for would-be wide-boys DelBoy and Rodney back in the '80s, then it was certainly good enough for Bruce Grobbelaar. Grob scored himself a nice little deal on the side. It even had an upgrade on the Trotter Independent Trading Company car's three wheels.

While interviewing keepers about their careers in nylon and latex, a suprising number of car stories have arisen. We covered Peter Mellor's

side job driving a Rolls-Royce for hire in *Glove Story*; we've since discovered that Phil Parkes' deal with a Wokingham garage saw

him take over sponsorship from none other than world champion racing driver James Hunt, and that Bryan Gunn was also once given a hand-me-down motor.

"I had a Rover at Aberdeen, and then at Norwich I got a Fiat Cromer which had been Steve Bruce's before he moved to United," Bryan admitted. "The Rover had a magnetic panel with my name and 'Morrison Painters & Decorators'. So if we went into town for the night, I could easily take it off and stick it in the boot. Not great advertising for them!"

But perhaps the best story was told to us by Tony Coton, from the time when he was number one at Manchester City. It's a vintage number wheeled out at many a

Brand loyalty is nothing new to uhlsport, but Sheffield United's international goalkeeper has taken the marketing term into a new dimension.

27-year old Alan, a member of Jack Charlton's Republic of Ireland World Cup squad, further cemented his relationship with the international brand, choosing the registration plate 'M97 UHL' for his stylish Land Rover Discovery.

Kelly – diving and driving with uhlsport.

sportsmen's dinner, but is still in excellent cond. with hardly any signs of wear and tear – even making an appearance in his must-read autobiography, *There To Be Shot At*.

Tony was dropped off at home by a chauffeur at five in the morning after a long-haul England trip to play in Russia.

whether he'd left the car somewhere else.

"So you think you've lost your car," the police operator said. "You can't find it, even though it's got your name on the door in foot-high letters..."

Within an hour the car had been tracked down to Wythenshawe. Hearing that the car was jacked up on bricks, Tony was worried that his cheque-book would be gone and his football gear distributed around the characterful local pubs. But he needn't have worried. He found a note on the steering wheel.

"Sorry TC, we only wanted the wheels. Hope this hasn't caused

In safe hands: Tony Godden's motor was sponsored by a local insurance company who were all big WBA supporters.

Tired out, he could neither find his keys nor remember whether his Sondico-sponsored XR3i should have been parked on the driveway. Maybe his wife had taken it to her mum's? In which case, where was her car?

In the morning, he found the tell-tale signs of broken glass, but still wasn't certain

you too much trouble 'cos we're City fans. Good luck, mate..."

23

PAT JENNINGS
SHEFFIELD WEDNESDAY 1-1
ARSENAL
Date: 6 January 1979
Venue: Hillsborough

On their way to winning the FA Cup in 1979 it took Arsenal five games to get past Sheffield Wednesday in the third round.

With the score at 1-0 to the Arsenal in the first match, the start of the second half was delayed due to snowballs raining down on Arsenal keeper Pat Jennings from the Kop end. When Owls boss Jack Charlton appealed to the fans to stop, he too then Kopped it in seasonal style.

Chris Turner was the keeper up the other end that day, and he tells us that he got off lightly from the Arsenal supporters, and wasn't subjected to the same treatment.

"We had five great games against them," Chris said, "and to play on the same pitch as big Pat was a privilege."

Even so, after three more thrilling draws and a final exit at neutral Filbert Street [I was there at every one! – Ed.] Chris was probably relieved to see the back of the Irish legend.

Jennings still kept his cool...

PICK UP THE PIECES

Without wishing to upset the feelgood vibe and positive karma associated with *Glove Story 2* so far, I feel slightly queasy at the very sight of this page.

Faced with the prospect of four enviable vintage jigsaws featuring goalies of yesteryear, I just found myself slipping helplessly back to circa 1972, and a sizeable collection of similar puzzles stuffed inside my wardrobe. They were given away with HP baked beans, I remember, and my sister just happened to know someone who worked for HP. So I was lucky enough to get several copies of each jigsaw.

Thing is, I just Googled the bloody things, and discovered

they're now highly collectable, worth up to £50 a pop on eBay. And I had all eight, including a smashing Peter Shilton from the goalkeeping fraternity.

Ah well, here's hoping you enjoy any rosy memories stirred up by the shattered perm of Toni Schumacher, by the unfinished clutching hands of Peter Shilton, by Frank Swift levitating for England or a '70s Waddington's Banksy that's

Toni's hairdon't looks a doddle, but that goalpost will be hard work...

now probably worth as much as an actual contemporary art Banksy.

It can surely only be me whose appreciation of the jigsaw was ruined forever when my mum kindly passed on my priceless puzzles to the kid next door at some point in the early '80s.

25

SAVE YOUR BREATH

It's a pun, see? The verb 'to save' doesn't only bring to mind balls not going into nets, but also describes pennies in a bank account. It's funny. It's memorable. And if it ain't broke, why mess with a winning formula?

There's only one thing safer than Alan Rough's pair of hands, and that's a bet on any advert that features a goalie also involving a long-forgotten regional building society or a fleetingly state-of-art photographic gimmick.

Legal note: other calf-skin coats and iffy team clocks are available.

Casual clash: Peter's sweater or Gary's Man U jacket?

KEEPERS OF THE SMALLER SCREEN

When it comes to television and goalkeepers, one of the most memorable performances came in 1999 when the Honey Monster saved a last-minute penalty at Wembley in a Sugar Puffs ad. Older readers may remember the antics of Harvey McGuinn

(Julian Walsh) between the sticks for the Glipton Grasshoppers in the BBC's seminal *Jossy's Giants* – while over on ITV was *Murphy's Mob*, featuring televised Watford games badly spliced with staged goals at Vicarage Road.

Of course, there have been many cameos down the years. Ray Clemence portrayed his own ancestor in *The Nearly Complete and Utter History of Everything*, and who can forget Bruce Grobbelaar making a fine save at the local recreation ground in one of the many fantasy sequences in Channel Four's *Scully*, which also saw Kenny Dalglish doused in red paint.

One gem to be unearthed is Chris Walker's portrayal of keeper Brian Rimmer in *The Manageress*. As the weather-beaten Second Division custodian at the heart of the Cherie Lunghi's defence, Rimmer was a part-time trumpet player in a band who – spoiler alert! – saves a last-minute penalty to secure the club's status in the top flight.

In the one-off drama *Eleven Men Against Eleven*, James Bolam starred as an ex-player brought in as caretaker manager at a desperate Premiership club. Here, none of the keepers in question cover themselves in glory. His first-choice custodian is a gambling addict and is arrested for match fixing. An opposition keeper tries to throw a game. And Bolam's club-legend status turns out to rest on a goal conceded by a goalie-turned-reporter who was paid £300 to throw the ball into his own net.

Back in the 1970s, David Bradley (*Game of Thrones, Doctor Who*) could be found diving in the mud while keeping goal for Parker Street in the one-off ITV drama, *Another Sunday and Sweet FA*. Written by Jack Rosenthal, the joys of amateur football were lovingly captured in a tapestry of ramshackle

changing rooms, wonky white lines and dodgy linesman. Bradley has a lovers' tiff with his girlfriend during the game and almost concedes a goal as a result. It's happened to the best of us, right?

Denley Moor Academicals' goalkeeper certainly had a story to tell the grandkids when he rushed out of his goal to get Neville Davitt's autograph back in 1935, having just

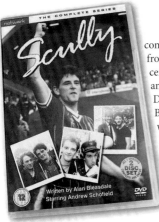

conceded a header from the bald centre forward and butcher. Davitt, star of Barnstone-worth United's 1922 Yorkshire Premier League winning side, had come out of retirement to lead his former team to an 8-1 victory in the Cup. Sorry. That should be "EIGHT-BLOODY-ONE". Gordon Ottershaw's desperate attempts to keep his club alive was certainly a ripping yarn. Charles McKeown played the hapless goalkeeper in Michael Palin's *Golden Gordon*, which is still arguably the greatest football-related television programme ever to be aired.

But running it damn close is *The World Cup: A Captain's Tale*, Tyne-Tees TV's glorious ode to the plucky exploits of West Auckland in the Lipton Trophy before the First World War. Aired prior to the start of the 1982 World Cup in Spain, it starred Dennis Waterman and Tim Healy as the backbone of a non-league side accidentally invited to take part in the competition instead of Woolwich Arsenal. The drama co-starred Dai 'Kes' Bradley, Richard 'Uncle Monty' Griffiths and a helmetless Boba Fett in the heart of

the midfield. But the player of interest is Auckland's goalkeeper Jimmy Dickenson, played by Scottish actor Ken Hutchinson in a pitch-perfect performance, resplendent in baggy shorts and an oversized flat cap.

Warned that he'll need "arms like an octopus" in the final against Juventus, Dickenson plays a blinder and even gets

to indulge in some Cantona-esque ill behaviour – one of few fictional additions to an amazing drama based on a true story.

With thanks to Neil Andrews at the excellent goalkeepersaredifferent.com

MAIER

Whenever the name of Josef Dieter 'Sepp' Maier is mentioned, you can't help but think of the revolutionary, oversized gloves that he was the first to popularise.

I remember the first World Cup I saw on TV back in 1978, and there were three things that made a huge impression on the goalkeeping front.

Firstly, there was Alan Rough's shaggy perm, undeniably fashionable at the time.

Then there was Peru's Ramón Quiroga scything down a Polish forward on the halfway line.

But far more important to my own future was the first time I saw Sepp Maier in a huge pair of gloves with a cool 'S' on the back.

While I subsequently managed to resist the schoolboy perm look and hacking down too many centre-forwards 50 yards from my goal line, those gloves proved personally irresistible, influential and utterly iconic.

Looking back, it seems strange to have to admit that I never spotted at the time what else was on the back of the gloves. It was only many years later that I was alerted to the second character stitched into the design detail – there wasn't just an 'S' on the backhand but also a cunningly disguised 'M' just below.

Speaking to *Champions* magazine in 2005, Sepp Maier talked about his reasoning behind wearing the gloves oversized.

"Tight gloves just didn't feel right," he reasoned on the physics of goalkeeping. "Large gloves are like a soft cushion for the ball so it won't rebound very far. Throw a tennis ball against a wall and watch how far it rebounds. Throw a tennis ball against a curtain, it drops to the ground almost vertically. Big gloves swallow velocity."

Sepp was a larger-than-life character who made close to 600 appearances for Bayern Munich (in fact, his frustrating final total of 599 could hardly have been closer) along with an impressive 95 starts for his country, which was then West Germany.

Despite not featuring in any games, he was part of the 1966 squad which lost to England at Wembley. Sadly, his career ended in 1979 due to a car crash in heavy rain, whilst driving to his home in Anzig. His injuries brought to an end Maier's astonishing run of 442 consecutive Bundesliga matches, comprising no less than 13 complete seasons.

Sepp later became

S and M: It's all too easy to miss the 'M' on Sepp's vintage mitts.

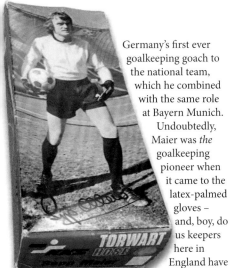

Germany's first ever goalkeeping goach to the national team, which he combined with the same role at Bayern Munich. Undoubtedly, Maier was *the* goalkeeping pioneer when it came to the latex-palmed gloves – and, boy, do us keepers here in England have a lot to thank him for. At a time when we were still wearing cotton gloves and Peter Bonetti table-tennis palm specials, all we could do was look on in envy and in awe.

Not only did he have a range of gloves with his name emblazoned on them, he also had jerseys, shorts and tracksuit bottoms. All with the famous Sepp Maier signature embroidered into the material.

When Sukan Sports produced their first four-page colour catalogue in 1982, the German keeper's influence was still going strong, and the Sepp Maier cotton extra-long-cut shorts were included along with his padded tracksuit trousers. However these must-have items were not cheap. The shorts were double the price of a pair of Gary Bailey's. In fact, at £25.95, the tracksuit trousers were the dearest item in the entire catalogue, costing the same as two pairs of Uhlsport 031s.

Dave Holmes of Sukan Sports first saw the Sepp Maier KKS range at Munich's ISPO international trade show, and ordered them direct from the manufacturer.

"Unfortunately, I don't speak German and had great difficulty in dealing with the company," he told us. "So at one stage I even wrote to Miss Stuch, my contact at Reusch, asking if she would be kind enough

to contact them on my behalf, in German. Sales were very good. We sold 71 pairs of the shorts and 122 pairs of the trousers, which I was very pleased with, and would have been happy to continue selling KKS products. But, in the end, the language and supply details were too difficult to overcome."

To put the demand for premium Sepp Maier gear in perspective, most UK sports shops only stocked a basic short with padding for goalkeepers, like the Star Gary Bailey, of which Sukan sold 256 pairs in that same 1982-83 season.

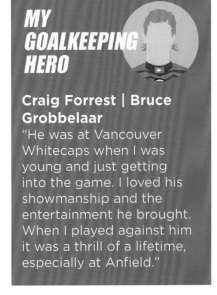

MY GOALKEEPING HERO

Craig Forrest | Bruce Grobbelaar

"He was at Vancouver Whitecaps when I was young and just getting into the game. I loved his showmanship and the entertainment he brought. When I played against him it was a thrill of a lifetime, especially at Anfield."

THE EVOLUTION OF THE GOALKEEPING COACH

Many of the first specialist goalkeeping coaches were ex-pros who turned their hands to passing on tips to the next generation. In the early days, they often operated on a part-time basis, travelling from club to club with balls and cones in the boot of their car. They would rarely be seen on matchdays warming up

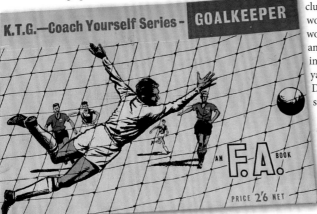

K.T.G.—Coach Yourself Series – GOALKEEPER

AN F.A. BOOK

PRICE 2'6 NET

the keepers, a task normally left to a rather bored substitute.

Times change, and it's now the norm for every professional club to have a specialist GK coach, often with a team of assistants working together to develop the skills and techniques of a group of youngsters. But it's a role that evolved very slowly and shockingly recently in comparison to outfield coaching.

In the late '60s, former Wolves & England keeper Bert Williams instituted a groundbreaking Goalkeeping School. Joe Corrigan has related the story that Malcolm Allison brought in Bert to work with him long before any other manager had thought of doing so:

"To listen to Bert's advice and have someone like that show you the ropes was awe inspiring, and it gave me a definite edge."

In *Glove Story*, Gordon Banks described how his training regime at Leicester chiefly

involved playing outfield in five-a-side matches on the Filbert Street car park. By the '70s, his successor Peter Shilton was faring only a little better along with his own eventual replacement, Mark Wallington.

"We didn't have a specialist goalkeeping coach," Mark recalls, "but fortunately for me Shilts was very conscientious about working on and analysing his own game, and that taught me an awful lot. The club coach, Dave Coates, would spend hour after hour working with us. If we wanted anything specific like, for instance, a shot to the left six yards out driven in low, then Dave could put a ball on a sixpence.

"But a lot of it was self analysis and Peter used to coach me and we used to help each other. He was magnanimous enough to say to me: 'Mark, do you think my position was right?' And we used to think an awful lot about the game. We got on very, very well. Obviously, a lot of the benefit came my way but we did used to help each other out."

By 1978, Manchester United finally took the plunge and employed their former Northern Iteland keeper Harry Gregg as a specialist goalkeeping coach.

In 1981, Alan Hodgkinson followed in the

Fig. 5a and b. Hands behind ball, and legs behind hands

Fig. 9. Catch the ball at the full height of your leap

same role at Coventry City, on a part-time basis under Dave Sexton. He also started coaching one day a week at Watford and Manchester City before becoming part-time goalkeeping coach to the England Under-18s and -21s. He later switched to join Andy Roxburgh in Scotland, combining this role as Manchester United's full-time GK coach under Sir Alex Ferguson.

By 1982, Peter Bonetti was Chelsea's part-time GK coach while slowly building a portfolio of other freelance roles at Watford, Birmingham, Coventry and Everton. That's where he helped produce the *Great Save!* coaching video with Neville Southall. In 1992 he was appointed England's senior GK coach on a part-time basis under Graham Taylor.

But England's first recognised senior goalkeeping coach and FA national schools GK coach was Mike Kelly, who held the post from 1984 to 1990, the first to attend two World Cups with England, at Mexico '86 and Italia '90.

By this time, most professional clubs finally had a goalkeeping coach in place, working on a part-time basis, maybe one or two days per week; but it was the mid '90s before they started to make full-time appointments.

Ray Clemence held the first senior full-time England position from 1998 to 2014; but it's incredible to think that it was only in the period 1999-2005 that the various recognised FA coaching certificates were finally introduced.

NEED, NEED, NEED

When we appeared on talkSport's terrific Hawksbee & Jacobs Show, chatting to the boys about *Glove Story*, that's when Paul Hawksbee simply couldn't stop himself blurting out, "It's goalkeeper glove porn!"

No matter if it was sold out 30 years ago, impossible to find or too dear, then and now. We don't just desire this stuff, we *need* it. *Pleease*, mum...

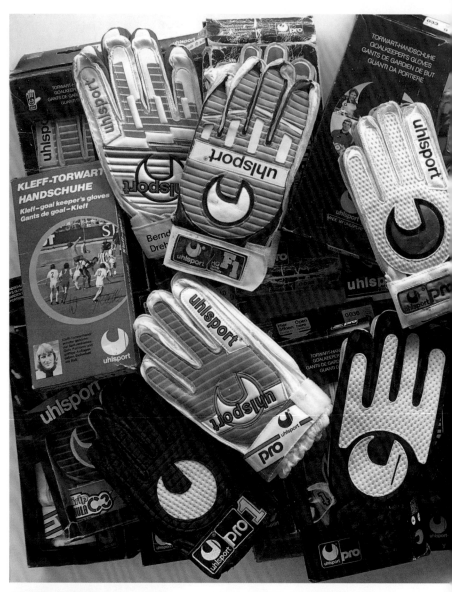

GLOVE BRAND: UHLSPORT

As glove brands go, Uhlsport has been at the forefront of keeping hands covered since the '70s. However, the history of the German company goes considerably further back, having been founded by Karl Uhl as a football boot component manufacturer in 1948, slowly branching out into other sporting protective wear.

Who knew that Uhlsport was yet another of

36

the great European sporting goods companies to have been named after its prime mover, like Karl Reusch's brainchild and the Italian brand named for the Fila dynasty; like Adolf Dassler's Adidas and, er, Patrice Beneteau's self-referential Patrick?

37

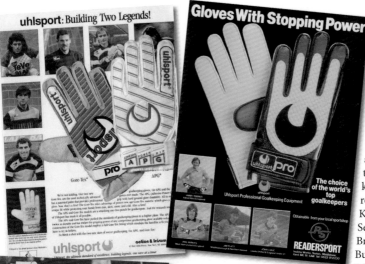

studs to share around their lucky deputies and team-mates.

The following year's catalogue in 1978 saw the addition of more top European keepers to the roster, including Karl Engel of Servette, Werder Bremen's Dieter Burdenski and FC Köln's Toni Schumacher. Tellingly, the latter had jumped ship from the heavily 'H'-emblazoned Heinze Sportartikel brand, which he memorably wore for the Cologne club against QPR in their UEFA Cup encounters in 1976.

A great leap forward came in 1979 with the introduction of the legendary Italian number one, Dino Zoff. He positively lit up the catalogue cover in his black and

Producing gloves in Germany's deep South-west region of Baden-Württemberg, the Uhlsport factories in Balingen, Grossel-fingen and Nagold tended to all the needs of the company's initial endorsee goalkeepers back in 1977.

Eintracht Braunschweig's Bernd Franke, together with Borussia Mönchengladbach's pair of Wolfgangs, Kleff and Kneib, took on the role of the brand's poster boys, capably backing up the marketing claim that Uhlsport gloves were "made by professionals for professionals."

With three factories churning out 12 different pairs of gloves, the Uhlsport keepers' glovebags must have been among the most enviably stuffed in the Bundesliga, with a growing range of jerseys, balls and

38

KLEFF-TORWART
HANDSCHUHE
Kleff-goal keeper's gloves
Gants de goal-Kleff

Kleff-Torwarthand-
schuhe gehören
zur Spitzenklasse.
Gute Paßform und
griffige Auflagen
geben Sicherheit
am Ball.

uhlsport

TORWARTHANDSCHUHE

0 1 9 5

white 025 gloves. And also included that landmark year was Jimmy Rimmer, who became the first English goalkeeper to be sponsored by Uhlsport.

With Jimmy on board, the profile of the brand was raised enormously here in the UK with adverts in *Shoot!* and *Match Weekly* whipping up big business most weeks.

Meanwhile, Jimmy himself was free to wear Uhlsport jerseys between the sticks for Aston Villa, even though the club was sponsored by Le Coq Sportif. At times, he even double branded his shirts with two Uhlsport logos. Subtle, see?

The Uhlsport 034 was one of the brand's most iconic products, which Rimmer and many others preferred

as their glove of choice. Pat Jennings notably sported them at two successive World Cups, while Dino Zoff wore them in the first half of the 1982 final before mysteriously switching to the 040 model for the second period.

Sukan Sports advertised the 034 in its initial one-page catalogue back in 1981 (see p.104). Remaining available right up until 1989, this design classic did take on a few tweaks here and there over the years, but the glove always

remained true to its unmistakable red, white and black colourway.

A glove supreme, for all seasons.

SUBBUTEO GOALKEEPERS

Purely by chance, the arrival of my first ever Subbuteo starter set one unforgettable Christmas morning gave me an extra-special thrill in the goalkeeping department.

In the 'Continental' Display Edition of the early 1970s, it must have been company

out every week for Leicester City sporting an eye-catching all-white 'PS'-branded strip. I used to look down on our very own super-safe shotstopper from the Olympus-like slopes of the old Double Decker at Filbert Street. The best goalkeeper in the world, obviously. And

here he was, in microscopic OO-scale detail, plonked by some 5,000-1 chance in my set of pick-up players in unfancied colours.

policy to use up players from random – or maybe the not quite so in-demand – boxed teams, as my set featured the rather unlikely Heavyweight combination of Exeter/Red Star Belgrade and Queens Park Rangers. It was Stripes versus Hoops, and I lined up both teams in the solid 3-2-5 formation of the day.

But it was between the sticks

Pete (as only I have ever been allowed to call him) lived and performed on the end of a thin wire rod, the same set-up that had

where my seemingly bespoke secret weapon resided. This was the time when Peter Shilton had done a deal with Admiral and turned

been used by Subbuteo since day one. Later on, I inherited a set of 'Interchangeable Goalkeepers' (set C133). And, would you

40

believe, there among the four diving and two standing options was another tiny Pete – the only goalie to date ever to have worn all

development of custom kicking and throwing keepers (C202/203). There was one on the cover of *Glove Story*. But don't worry, they didn't actually throw or kick. You just subbed them on for a few seconds like an American football kicker. Not a patch on my little Pete.

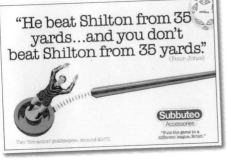

white, in among the red, blue, yellow, green and black hoi-palloi.

The next team sets I got for my birthday included the blue-and-white Heavyweights of Leicester City, though now the goalie rod had evolved into green plastic.

You could even transfer in special goalies with caps (C153), and 'live-action' keepers on springs with a 45-minute life expectancy (C123); but this was long before the '80s

INTERCHANGEABLE

GOALKEEPERS

(REGD DESIGN)

SUBBUTEO TABLE SOCCER

Four Diving and Two Standing Goalkeepers with new style (2) Interchangeable Rods in six different colours.

by
SUBBUTEO

Memorable GOALKEEPING No 2 MOMENTS

JAN TOMASZEWSKI
ENGLAND 1-1 POLAND
Date: 17 October 1973
Venue: Wembley Stadium

ITV nabbed the live rights to this must-win night match on England's unstoppable march to the 1974 World Cup finals. And just to add extra spice, they invited along Brian Clough as a pundit, fresh from his resignation as Derby boss just two days previously. At half-time Cloughie refused to back down on his description of Tomaszewski as a 'clown': "Keep calm. Put the kettle on, mother. Don't worry – the goals are going to come."

Of course, Jan went on to have the game of his life in a pair of Coffer Sports' Gordon Banks gloves. Maybe Shilton could have fared better in them if he hadn't opted for the black woollen option? On his infamous, costly gaffe, Shilton said: "I tried to make the perfect save. Had I been more experienced, I'd have stuck a foot or knee out."

Tomaszewski went on to be voted the goalkeeper of the 1974 World Cup finals as Poland finished third, beating Brazil in the third/fourth play-off.

That man is a clown...

SHINPADS FOR SHOTSTOPPERS

Not a lot of people know the name of Sam Weller Widdowson; but if you've ever gone sliding sideways through the mud in a one-on-one against a burly psycho of a centre-forward, then you might like to thank old Sam retrospectively for that dull ache you felt in your lower leg. If it hadn't been for his Victorian ingenuity, your angry bruise could easily have been a shattered shinbone. And they've been known to smart a bit.

Some 150 years ago, Nottingham Forest footballer Widdowson chopped down the cricket pads he wore for Nottinghamshire and attached them to his legs, on the outside of his woolly socks, using leather straps.

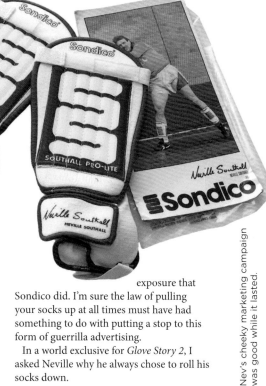

My, how the other players laughed. But Sam's comical DIY padding was now a thing. And the rest, as they say, was shinpads.

When it came to pads for the exclusive use of goalkeepers, the great Neville Southall of Everton and Wales surely deserves a considerable share of Sam's praise.

Neville made advertising shinpads an art for Sondico Sports, with his socks rolled down and the company's big 'double S' logo boldly on display.

Other glove brands such as Uhlsport and Reusch did make shinners, but never got the amount of exposure that Sondico did. I'm sure the law of pulling your socks up at all times must have had something to do with putting a stop to this form of guerrilla advertising.

In a world exclusive for *Glove Story 2*, I asked Neville why he always chose to roll his socks down.

"I had a back nerve problem at the time," he explained, "which meant the socks irritated my legs badly. In hindsight, I should have asked for more money from them."

Nev's cheeky marketing campaign was good while it lasted.

43

Shoot! magazine, May 1985: "Everton's superstar goalkeeper Neville Southall has no excuse for being late for training – he has more than 30 clocks in his Woolton home!"

Remembering this gem of informaation from back in the day, we thought it would make the perfect ice-breaker. Whenever Nev went away with Everton or Wales, he always brought home his wife a clock as a present. By now, his collection must be well into the thousands?

"Sorry, no," says Nev. "I never collected clocks. Sadly, that isn't true."

Aha. So much for the importance of research. But what about your classic matchworn shirts and gloves? What memories you must have stashed away!

"I was never a collector," Neville deadpans. "I never kept anything".

But surely, having worn all the top glove brands – Uhlsport, Reusch, Sondico, even Mitre – you must have a favourite?

"To be honest, I liked all the gloves I wore all at different times, so there wasn't one that was a particular favourite."

Moving swiftly on... let's run with a bit of background. Neville was famously a hod carrier on building sites while playing for Winsford in the Cheshire League, where at the age of 22 he was picked up by Bury. So it was 1980 when he experienced his first taste of proper goalkeeping coaching. Every Tuesday afternoon, former Man United boss Wilf McGuinness would take him for a session. And 39 appearances later he was signed for Everton by Howard Kendall – as an understudy to Jim Arnold, mind, who had just cost £150K from Blackburn Rovers.

In the early days he would often go and watch Liverpool play, just to study Bruce Grobbelaar; but Nev was hardly a traitor to the Blue cause, remaining at Everton until 1998, clocking up (no, don't mention clocks!) a cool 578 appearances.

After just one first-team start, he was called up to the Wales squad by Mike England and went on to replace Dai Davies as the undisputed Welsh number one.

Nev admits his boyhood heroes were Pat Jennings, Gordon Banks and Peter Bonetti, and the latter pair went on to become his coaches after they finished playing. He even made a video with Bonetti: *Great Save!* was filmed at Everton's training ground, and included a guest appearance from top pop personality Gary

44

Christian. Yes, him out of the Christians.

Yet it was Pat Jennings that Nev admired most: "He was different to the other keepers as he could save the ball with any part of

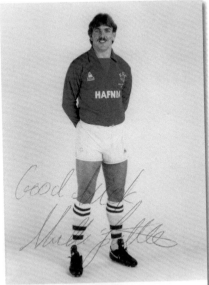

Neville Southall
Everton and Wales International Goalkeeper

so many fans claim.

Nev expounds on this stop in his autobiography, *The Binman Chronicles:* "Glenn Hoddle crossed the ball into the area and from point-blank range Mark Falco headed it towards my top corner. I stretched for it and tipped it over the crossbar. What more can I say? It was straight at me, and I'd saved plenty like that on the training ground. I always knew I was going to get it."

However, despite the rapturous applause from the travelling Evertonians, Kevin Ratcliffe yelled, "Why didn't you catch it? Why are you f****** giving away a corner?"

Who said feedback can be harsh for keepers on social media, these days?

his body, and always seemed to be in the right place at the right time, where other goalkeepers at this time were a bit robotic to me."

We were going to ask Neville about Howard Kendall's first impressions – "The thing that struck me about him was that in physique he resembled Jimmy Rimmer. In terms of talent, he can be a second Peter Shilton" – but that was reported in *Shoot!* and we can't risk another fumble!

Best stick to facts and report that Neville was awarded the Football Writers' POTY Award in 1985, being the fourth and last goalkeeper to do so. That season he produced two saves which are still talked about today. The save from Sheffield Wednesday's Imre Varadi even made the opening titles for the following season's *Match of the Day*, and the other won Everton the title at Tottenham – or

MY GOALKEEPING HERO

**Shaka Hislop |
Ray Clemence & Joe Corrigan**
"We used to have a TV programme each week in Trinidad called 'The Road to Wembley' and these two always stood out for me."

The PL's last
recorded
sighting of
mud and rain:
Old Trafford,
April 1997.

THESE THINGS WERE SENT TO TRY US No 1: Mud

They don't know they were blinkin' well born, this current generation of Premier League keepers.

I remember the day when the only grass to be found on a football pitch was down by the corner flags, and by September the goalmouths at every ground in the country were two or three inches thick with slippery, stinking mud, straight out of the trenches.

They don't even play on grass these days, it's all soft green plastic carpets. Even if it were allowed to rain on a top-flight pitch, it would never cut up into proper mud. And, to think, a goalie used to be in his element in thick brown slime.

What chance these days of a penalty spot going missing in a puddle the size of the 18-yard box? Big Joe Corrigan was only too happy to help out as the bucket of white paint and big brush were brought forth.

"Do it about 14 yards out, mate."

GLOVE BRAND: REUSCH

It would be easy to fill up a whole spread with the names of notable goalkeepers who have pulled on the latex-palmed gloves of Reusch. Starting with five World Cup winners – Fillol (Argentina '78), Pumpido (Argentina '86), Illgner (Germany '90), Taffarel (Brazil '94) and Reis (Brazil '02) – the list of greats is endless. Schmeichel, Maier, Van Breukelen,

Meola, Dida, Auhmann, Galli, Buffon, Enke, Campos, Immel, Pfaff, Schumacher...

Fillol, however, is in disputed waters, as for most of the tournament he wore Heinze, only opting for Reusch in an early group match.

Elsewhere, in a strange grey area between brands, our research reveals Dino Zoff (Italy) and Leao (Brazil) being featured in Reusch's 1978 World Cup brochure, wearing Adidas-

branded Curkovic gloves! The simple explanation is that Reusch made other companies' gloves for many years.

In the UK, Reusch endorsees included the likes of Chris Woods, Dave Beasant, Eddie Niedzwiecki,

Martin Thomas and Dai Davies in a similarly exhaustive roll-call. And, once again, there in the Reusch brochure for 1983/84 are Peter Shilton and Alan Rough wearing Coffer and Umbro, respectively.

Other brands used Reusch in their 1977/78 catalogue.

It's important to note that keepers of the late '70s early '80s, especially here in the UK, weren't paid to endorse gloves but were just happy to get a limited number for free.

for manufacturing because of the quality of materials available. We believe they even made the odd pair for Uhlsport, including the inside-stitched 023 glove that first appeared

Bristol Rovers youngster Martin Thomas used his initiative to become an early wearer of the Reusch brand in the late '70s.

"On the keepers' grapevine I heard about the new German gloves," he

Below: Coffer and Umbro in a Reusch catalogue!

Sukan a few years later, and by this time I had moved to Newcastle and this meant I got unlimited gloves but no money. When we got promoted to the old First Division in 1984 I signed an agreement at £500 per year plus gloves, leisurewear and equipment. I

told us, "and then managed to get contact details for Reusch in Metzingen. I wrote to them and asked about their range, and they sent me catalogues and prices. I used to order the gloves direct.

"When Dave Holmes started Sukan Sports he got in contact and said they'd be distributing Reusch products moving forward. Dave kindly supplied my gloves free of charge – six pairs a season, which included an advert in the match programme.

"Reusch UK took over the agreement from

even managed to get the wife to iron a Reusch transfer on to my jersey as the rules then on goalkeepers jerseys and advertising were very relaxed!"

BRING BACK THE BACKPASS

As wrong as it feels to round on a fully paid up member of the Goalkeepers' Union, it's hard not to get a delicious sensation of *schadenfreude* watching the final, decisive moments of the Scotland-Wales match in the 1978 Home International series.

You can't blame Coventry City's Jim Blyth, who was between the sticks for Scotland that night at Hampden Park. He only did what any keeper would have done at the time, running down the clock in criminal but then legal fashion, with his own side protecting a 1-0 lead they'd had since the tenth minute.

In the final minute of the match, Gordon Strachan tapped a free-kick on the edge of the box back into the hands of Blyth, who duly bowled it out to Aberdeen's Stuart Kennedy in the right-back berth. Who promptly booted it straight back to Blyth. You get the picture. It's obvious what

'Safe Hands'... and here he pings a defence-splitting pass 75 yards, to feet.

happened next: he picked up the ball and rolled it out to Man City's Willie Donachie, trotting back into the left-back position. And, inevitably, Donachie toe-poked the ball straight back to Blyth. This could have

DOUBLE TROUBLE

David Seaman will need an operation on a double hernia in the summer – all because of the new back-pass law.

Jerry Gimore, an expert on groin injuries, explains: "Extra strain has been put on 'keepers because of the change. They've caught up with outfield players in injuries."

gone on indefinitely – or at least until the final whistle. Except Donachie happened to catch the ball rather cleanly with his time-wasting poke back into the area, and Blyth wasn't quite ready for what amounted to a tantalisingly slow, spinning shot at goal.

In the commentators' box, Hugh Johns was having eggs: "Oh... oh... an *own-goal* by Willie Donachie! That's the most *remarkable* goal that's ever been scored, surely, here at Hampden. Donachie, who's never scored for Scotland, *has now scored for Wales!*"

Although Jim Blyth travelled with the Scotland squad to the imminent World Cup, he never again pulled on the hallowed yellow nylon, adding to that horribly forgettable second cap.

So, let's just say it wasn't *every* British goalkeeper who viewed the new backpass law of 1992 with paranoid suspicion and extreme trepidation.

Introduced in order to stamp out the time-wasting, ultra-defensive shenanigans that had besmirched Italia '90 and the 1992 Euros, the new law was good news for fans and for most neutral onlookers. But this was a law change that brought a whole new dimension to the goalkeeper's role. It demanded a previously unimaginable level of fancy footwork. No longer was

52

PENALTY PICK UP

the humble goalie able to pick up the ball at any time. Faced with a bobbling, skittering backpass from a pressurised centre-half, we were expected to calmly trap the ball and ping it out 40 yards to feet. We were no longer just the final line of defence but also the first line of attack. And should that fleet-footed forward charge past our back line and bear down like a ravenous lion on a timid, luminous wildebeest, we were supposed to drop a shoulder, give them the eyebrows, feint to the left and emerge in yards of space – hopefully with the ball still safely in our possession.

Suddenly, we were all required to become one of those exotic beasts – a footballer.

We asked some of our goalkeeping heroes what they thought of the new law back in 1992. And, let's not forget, these were the days of bobbly pitches, mud, puddles and sand everywhere. None of the snooker-table surfaces that today's sweeper-keepers can enjoy (with all due respect to Peter Enckleman, Paul Robinson and others who, like Jim Blyth, now have a sorry association with the dreaded backpass).

"Before the backpass rule," David Seaman confided, "me and Lee Dixon used to love running the clock down and wasting time when we were winning! Sadly, the new rule put a stop to that. I did find it hard, to be honest, especially when it got knocked back to me on my left foot. At the end of that first season, I ended up in hospital with Tony Adams, having hernia operations. Mine was a double one, too!"

Had Pompey's Alan Knight welcomed the changes? "No, not really! The backpass then wasn't really about encouraging teams to play from the back, it was more a case of hitting row Z of the North Stand for me. Let's just say it wasn't one of my strengths!"

But not all keepers struggled with the need

FIFA's new rule banning goalkeepers from handling back passes next season sounds like a recipe for disaster.

JASON FOLEY,
NEWMARKET, CAMBS.

But at least it will force defenders to play football instead of always taking the easy option. Too many defenders just hoof the ball back from the halfway line the minute they come under any sort of pressure. It's the reason our defenders always look out of their depth at international level. If it raises standards and makes the game more exciting, I'm all for it.

to adapt and evolve. Craig Forrest (Ipswich Town & Canada) told us: "It wasn't as bad as I thought it would be. I trained playing out enough to be somewhat comfortable with it." and good old John Burridge wasn't fazed for a moment: "I was comfortable with it when they introduced the new rule. I spent a lot of time playing football tennis and squash which really helped me and, to be honest, I enjoyed the challenge."

Personally, I used to love that early pass back to the keeper straight from the kick-off. Ahh, the good old days! It was great to get a good feel of the ball and make sure the gloves

Gary Neville scores his second goal for England, unfortunately at the wrong end...

were giving a good grip. That was something that Jimmy Rimmer took to extremes. I remember noticing him when I went to Wembley to watch Aston Villa v Spurs in the 1982 Charity Shield. I was more interested in watching Jimmy changing his gloves every five minutes than watching the match, much to my dad's frustration!

53

Memorable GOALKEEPING MOMENTS

No 3

JOHN BURRIDGE
Date: Before the big match
Venue: Every ground in England!

"Home games at Palace would start with a warm-up at 10am on the pitch, much to the groundsman's displeasure," Budgie confides. "Then I'd go home and back to bed for a couple of hours, and come back for the game. For away games we'd find some local pitches we could use. One time I even used a traffic island as there was nothing else available!

"My first on-pitch warm-up was at Old Trafford, late 1979. I was going out on to the pitch half an hour before kick-off, but I was stopped by the groundsman. He said, 'You're not going out there, kicking balls. We don't allow that here.' I said, 'Can I go out without a ball, then?' He said, 'OK, but stay out the goalmouths.' So out I went and did some running across the pitch in front of the Stretford End. I was getting a bit of stick, so I then started walking on my hands and doing a few back-flips and handstands. After that, I did it every week. People called me bonkers and mad, but I wanted to make sure I was in the best shape possible, ready for the game."

THE GOALIE GAME GRAIL

If you've ever read any of our previous books, you may recognise the name of top contributor Paul Woozley, who runs the fantastic OldFootballGames.com website. Paul is a world-renowned collector and expert on... you guessed it. And we've been lucky enough to spend a day round his house, helping him test out his vintage toys and games. You don't just

Pat's legendary all-action football game!

In short, Flik-Shot is better than Subbuteo and Striker and Fifa 21, all rolled into one. The little plaggy figures literally come alive when you stick on the kit of the Home International sides.

At least, that how it seemed to Paul when he clapped eyes on the game after a frustrating 30 years on its trail. In football

play with historical artefacts, right?

When Spurs fan Paul told us about his ultimate holy grail, you'll know how keen we were to help find one for him. Paul had only ever seen the adverts for Pat Jennings' Flik-Shot game from when it was given away with a Trebor comp in the early '70s. But real effort was involved in getting the game. Take-up was low. It ended up being so rare, we weren't even sure any had survived.

So imagine our surprise when we were rooting through a cache of photos we'd taken at the National Football Collection HQ, a staggering treasure trove of priceless relics and collectables – and came across these pics of

collector circles, they don't call us 'Sherlock' for nothing.

Or 'slightly forgetful'.

55

Choose your heroes wisely and they'll last you a lifetime. "My dad fought in World War I and lost two sons, Jock and Billy, two of my four brothers, in World War II," Bob Wilson told us. "He wasn't exactly enamoured by my choice of hero. Understandable of course, but I only wish Dad could have met Bert [Trautmann] as I was privileged to do. A guy who chose to stay in this country and help rebuild it post-war as well as winning not just memorable football matches, but the hearts of our nation."

Above: Paul Cooper of Ipswich Town with Jez Grimwood and his brother Scott.

Left: QPR's Peter Hucker and Stephen Brown (left), on the Loftus Road Omniturf.

Facing page: Aberdeen's Jim Leighton and Gordon Strachan with Eddie Hyslop in April 1983.

Right: Eric Steele, Chris Woods and GK Coach Dave Thompson - with Eddie Repton and his mate Luis Otten.

Above: Mark Crossley of Nottingham Forest and Kelly Isaacs.

Below: Dean Kiely of Portsmouth with Tom King, now first-team keeper at Newport County.

Above: Peter Shilton with Jonathan Swain, now a roving reporter on ITV's *GMTV*.

Left: Nottingham Forest's Hans Van Breukelen and Darren Wheater-Lowe.

Right: Pat Jennings with future Arsenal first-team keeper Alan Miller.

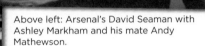

Above left: Arsenal's David Seaman with Ashley Markham and his mate Andy Mathewson.

Above: Ray Clemence with Stephen Monaghan, in Amsterdam 1977 for Liverpool's pre-season games v Ajax and Barcelona.

Left: Internazionale's Walter Zenga with Renato Marana.

Below left: Neville Southall of Everton, with Dean Thornton.

Below: Bob Wilson with Alan Walker-Harris at one of Bob's goalkeeping weeks.

Above: Erik Thorstvedt with Jeff Maysh. "My dad let me bunk off school to watch the Spurs keepers train."

Below: Portsmouth's Alan Knight with Luke Wheeler, receiving his Player of the Season trophy.

Above: Portsmouth's Peter Mellor with Roger Watling, guarding a doorway.

Below: Peter Bonetti of Chelsea with Chris Bignell in 1971.

59

RUDI HIDEN

When Austria played England in May 1930 and emerged from the match with a 0-0 draw thanks to the heroics of 21-year-old keeper Rudi Hiden, fans carried him high on their shoulders. We spoke to David Hermann-Meng, author of the acclaimed *Rudi Hiden* biography, to find out more about this legendary keeper – and why his proposed big-money transfer to Arsenal never took place.

Is it true that Arsenal manager Herbert Chapman wanted to sign Hiden?

"Yes, it was reported that he had set his heart on signing this wonderful young keeper. Two months after the game in Austria, Chapman offered WAC (Wiener Athletik Sport Club) £2,600 for his signature, and even offered him a job as a cook. But the strict Ministry of Labour restrictions on foreign footballers stopped it."

Wasn't he prevented from entering the UK?

"On 21st July Hiden started his train journey from Vienna to Calais in France, but he wasn't allowed to get an entry permit or a ferry to Dover. He was waiting for weeks in the Belgium port of Ostende to travel to Dover. The FA and the PFA were totally strict and didn't want players from outside the UK. Rudi tried three times to come to Dover, but he wasn't successful. Hiden told in his memoires that even the foreign minister, Arsenal fan Arthur Henderson, wanted to help him, but without success. Even Chapman tried to get a work permit, but on 17th August Hiden returned to Vienna."

After he joined RC Paris in 1933 there was a series of friendlies between Paris and Arsenal...

"Those Armistice Day games were first played in 1930 to benefit wounded victims of the First World War. Hiden played in the game in 1933. Arsenal won 1-0 in Park des Princes, but Hiden did a good job and was the best man on the pitch."

Did he ever get to play in England?

"Yes, he played in the famous England-Austria game in December 1932 at Stamford Bridge. In Austria, it was seen for a long time as the game of the century, even though Austria lost 4-3. The Austrian press wrote in detail about the game, the travel to London; it was broadcast outside in Vienna, where thousands of people listened to the game despite the cold. George, Duke of Kent; Edward, the Prince of Wales and many other prominent people watched that game. But Austria's Wonderteam series of 14 unbeaten games ended here."

Next, Hiden became a French national...

"On 1st May 1937 he gained French citizenship. Because the number of foreign

David Herrmann-Meng

Rudi Hiden
Die Hand des Wunderteams

Leykam

players was limited to two in Ligue 1, Racing Paris arranged some French passports." Are there any details about his military

service for France in World War II?

"A lot of players had to go to the front during the war. At first, Hiden was a coach for the soldiers at the Maginot Line. He trained with them, helping to get them into condition. In 1940, when Hitler's troops invaded Paris, Hiden was sent to a Gestapo prison in Trier, Germany. Because he'd become a French citizen, the Nazis saw him as a traitor. Later he was in Gestapo prison in Köln. But he was never beaten. Then he went to Paris, where he wrote for the *Pariser Zeitung* National Socialist newspaper. He wrote apolitical stuff about sports; he wasn't political at all. In 1944 he was in prison again, this time because of his association with the newspaper. But he simply didn't have any money. In court he was acquitted."

After the war, he coached in Italy...

"He came back to Austria as a sick man, without money, in 1968. In Italy he wasn't so successful, he even had to do a job as

a kind of 'Penalty Clown' in the Austrian circus, to get money. He didn't have Austrian citizenship any more, he didn't have enough to have a normal life. He was living from alms. He was often in hospital because his right leg was giving him problems, and finally it was amputated; he'd been a heavy smoker all his life. Newspapers collected money to help him out of his terrible situation.

"He wasn't able to pay for his prosthesis, his flat or anything. At the end of his life in 1970 he regained Austrian citizenship, but he was a broken man at that time. He died in Vienna on 11th September 1973."

MY GOALKEEPING HERO

Hans Van Breukelen | Jan van Beveren

"Jan van Beveren, PSV and Holland, was my idol/hero. A type like Lev Yashin, an athlete, looked very natural, great reflexes, great style. Brave too, and demanding in the box. I called him the Johan Cruyff of the goalkeepers. Because of a fight with Cruyff he only played 32 times for Holland and missed two World Cup finals in '74 and '78. A real shame. In 1982 he moved to the USA and played for Fort Lauderdale. A very nice person, too. He never got the recognition he deserved."

THE 'S' GLOVES

From Sepp Maier to Peter Schmeichel, the 'S' gloves were an iconic option taken up by many keepers over the years – and not always by those that had an 'S' in their names!

We asked Dave Holmes of Sukan Sports how he introduced the style into his range.

"The Reusch 024 'S' glove was in their range as a stock line, so in theory stocks were easy to get," Dave recalled. "And I'd seen the 'S' on the Sepp Maier gloves prior to us opening; but more importantly they told me that it

would be used by Toni Schumacher, and therefore they would be giving it a lot of promotion. Paul Cooper of Ipswich Town was already using the glove here in England, and I liked the way that it was distinctive and showed up well on TV and in photos. The deciding factor was that the 'S' could relate to Sukan Sports, so everything just seemed to fall into place."

PLASTIC PASSION

It was back in 1982 that I had my own first experience of playing on a plastic pitch, at Alexandra Park in Portsmouth. On the positive side, the adoption of Astroturf would mean fewer games postponed due to bad weather. And that's about it, from a goalie's perspective. The plastic pitch was effectively just a large outdoor carpet, and despite your tracksuit trousers, knee and elbow pads, you knew you'd be going home with bloodied knees, and suffering bruises for days.

But what about the professionals' view of the new invention that was potentially about to replace grass pitches across the country? We now know there were only ever a handful of plastic pitches used in the British Leagues; but optimism was high when they first came on to our radar.

"I'm standing on Europe's very first outdoor Astroturf football pitch," beamed *Blue Peter*'s Peter Purves back in 1972. And there he was in Islington, on a council pitch that had cost a cool £190K to lay. Peter explained that the surface was named after the artificial grass in the Houston Astrodome (not a lot of people know that, fact fans), and that it was made from three layers: grass-like 'nylon blades', a waterproof polyester section and a shock-absorbing rubber/vinyl pad.

But far more interestingly, he'd invited along as testers Crystal Palace's Bobby twins, Kellard and Tambling – along with QPR goalie Phil Parkes.

"I'd be very wary of wearing studs which might slip," Phil gave his first impressions. "I'm wearing flat trainers at the moment and it seems very good." But what about the possibility of burns? "I'd be wary of that to start with, but I don't think it could burn worse than a very hard or frosty ground." Phil then proceeded to dive like a playful dolphin on the new surface. Not all bad, then.

Entirely by coincidence, in 1981, QPR became the first club to install an artificial pitch in England – technically, not Astroturf but the product of a company called Omniturf. I asked the Superhoops' own Peter Hucker for his memories from this time, and whether he ever grew to like the plastic pitch. "Ha ha," he replied. "How could you ever like something that ripped your skin to bits, jarred every joint in your body and burned the skin on your knees and hips so much that you went home with a large tub of Flamazine after every game? That was the stuff that was used to treat burns victims in the Falklands...

"I needed new gloves after every game, which was fine when I was in the first team and had a sponsorship deal with Sondico Sports; however, when I was in the reserves, Budgie used to give me gloves for free, which helped. The speed of the ball off a wet surface doubled. It was a nightmare at times. The bounce was true, so we didn't have to endure nasty divots like when we played away, and most through-balls ran away from the strikers, so there were less one-on-one situations.

"The only good thing I can say about it was that John Burridge refused to

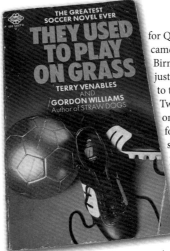

for QPR: "The club came in for me after Birmingham had just got relegated to the old Division Two. I knew it was only going to be for one season so it wasn't a problem as it meant I was back playing in the First Division.

It wasn't a great surface to play on. Everything I wore had to be padded, and even with all that gear on you could still feel it when you landed on it, mind."

Trust Neville Southall to take a different route from all the rest. Unbelievably, Nev took to wearing shorts when playing at Boundary Park against Oldham.

"The reason was," he explained to us, "the tracksuit bottoms restricted my movements and stopped me sliding across the pitch easily, so I just greased the thighs and knees with Vaseline and went out and played!"

BURRIDGE'S NIGHTMARE

QPR 'keeper John Burridge, on loan to Wolves, definitely won't be going back to Loftus Road. And he isn't looking forward to playing for anyone at the QPR ground.

Burridge said: "Playing on the artificial turf was causing me to have sleepless nights. I had half a season with Rangers playing on that surface and I knew it was not helping my game.

"I know my capabilities and my consistency was not being helped by the Loftus Road surface."

play on it and ended up leaving the club, so giving me my first team break!"

Over to Budgie now for his exclusive views:

"I hated it!"

David Seaman told us the plastic problem wasn't enough to put him off signing

Chris Guy (@retroQPR) with sister Tracy on the Superhoops' newly laid magic carpet. Great shot by dad Steve.

65

BERT TRAUTMANN
MAN CITY 3-1 BIRMINGHAM CITY
Date: 5 May 1956
Venue: Wembley Stadium

When Manchester City's German goalkeeper was named FWA Footballer of the Year two days before the 1956 FA Cup final, he appeared to have entered sporting history.

Having first played in goal in a World War II Prisoner of War camp, the former Nazi paratrooper was finally adopted by the forgiving city of Manchester, where he had arrived with some attendant controversy via local Lancashire side St Helens Town.

With 17 minutes to go at Wembley, City were leading Blues 3-1. A dangerous ball into the box then saw Trautmann launch a fearless headlong dive at the feet of striker Peter Murphy. Knocked unconscious by Murphy's knee, the goalkeeper looked distinctly groggy as the spongeman held up fingers and supported his aching neck.

But just short minutes later, in an era long before substitutes, Bert opted bravely to carry on – and was soon back in the thick of the action, making two key saves as City held on for the remainder of the match.

Only three days later did Trautmann get his newly crooked neck checked out, discovering that it had been broken in the final.

The toughest goalkeeper ever...

THE WRONG JERSEY

The first time Peter Shilton was supposed to wear his yellow/green and black zig-zag kit was at England's first Euro 88 game against the Republic of Ireland. However, due to concerns over a clash with the emerald shirts of Jack Charlton's side, Shilton felt a change was best; but, amazingly, no proper alternative had been brought and he ended up wearing his silver 1986 World Cup shirt.

For a keeper as fastidious about his appearance as Shilton, it was a far from ideal state of affairs, and a blue variant of that zig-zag kit came into use in 1989. However, that didn't mean the end of his problems, as he revealed in his autobiography.

"In 1984 [sic], I played for England against Scotland at Hampden. Arriving in the dressing room an hour or so before kick-off, I was taken aback to see the kit I'd been issued contained a dark blue jersey. I pointed out to Bobby Robson that I couldn't wear it because Scotland would be in their traditional dark blue shirts.

"No alternative jersey could be found, and so in the end I walked out at Hampden alongside the Scotland goalkeeper, Jim Leighton, the pair of us sporting yellow [more grey than yellow] goalkeeper's jerseys, complete with Scotland badge on the breast. That must be the only instance of an England goalkeeper wearing a Scotland shirt when playing against Scotland. It was pointless me swapping shirts with Jim after that game!"

You might think that the demand for shirt borrowing at international level was almost nil, but Shilton wasn't even the first England custodian to have to do so in the 1980s. At the beginning of the decade, Admiral-clad England were in Bucharest to face Romania and nobody thought to pack anything other than yellow goalkeeper shirts.

In the Under-21 game, John Lukic wore a plain blue top while in the senior clash Ray Clemence borrowed a green and black Adidas top from the hosts, identical to that worn by his opposite number Vasile Iordache.

England haven't been the only nation afflicted – in 1994, Neville Southall took to the field for Wales against Norway wearing a Cardiff City shirt, complete with *South Wales Echo* sponsorship, due to a clash. Conversely, Wales had been the shirt donors in May 1979 when the German kit man was found lacking and Sepp Maier walked out in Cardiff wearing red. For the first half, Maier wore the same yellow Admiral top as Dai Davies, but at least the visitors did find a properly badged option for the second half.

Wearing red against similarly clad opponents was also a trap that Jim Leighton fell into in 1983, when Switzerland visited Hampden Park. Though Scotland had no Umbro backup available, they did at least benefit from the fact that Queens Park also played at the home of Scottish football, meaning a Bukta top was able to be sourced.

With thanks to Denis Hurley at MuseumofJerseys.com

Shilts stops shots for Scots shock?!?

67

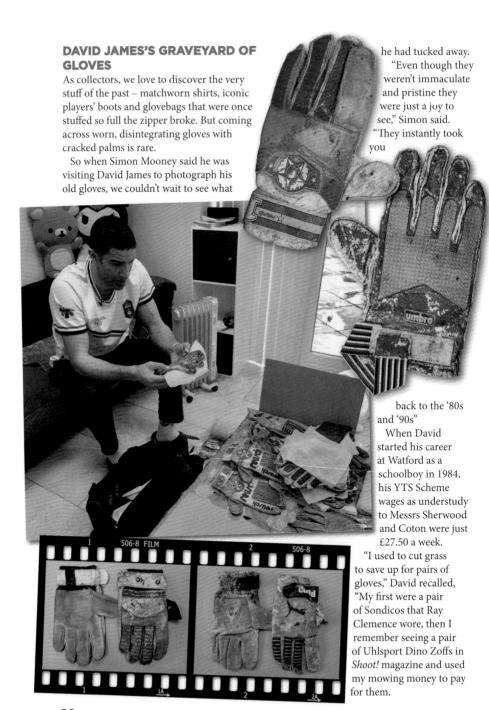

DAVID JAMES'S GRAVEYARD OF GLOVES

As collectors, we love to discover the very stuff of the past – matchworn shirts, iconic players' boots and glovebags that were once stuffed so full the zipper broke. But coming across worn, disintegrating gloves with cracked palms is rare.

So when Simon Mooney said he was visiting David James to photograph his old gloves, we couldn't wait to see what he had tucked away.

"Even though they weren't immaculate and pristine they were just a joy to see," Simon said. "They instantly took you back to the '80s and '90s"

When David started his career at Watford as a schoolboy in 1984, his YTS Scheme wages as understudy to Messrs Sherwood and Coton were just £27.50 a week.

"I used to cut grass to save up for pairs of gloves," David recalled, "My first were a pair of Sondicos that Ray Clemence wore, then I remember seeing a pair of Uhlsport Dino Zoffs in *Shoot!* magazine and used my mowing money to pay for them.

"Before my Watford debut in 1990 I didn't have a glove contract, so I got myself a pair of Adidas, which spent a couple of months at Watford.

"The Umbro gloves were provided by Watford as they were our kit manufacturer. I was buzzing when I was given the Bruce Grobbelaar colourway, but they were too big. I'd still use them until the fingers wore out!

"The Cannonballs were given to me by Dave Bassett, through his connection to Dave Beasant.

"Tony Coton let me have a few of his Reusch gloves, initially after I'd washed an old pair I found in the boot room. My first contract was with Puma, just after Tony Meola had gone back to the US. I wanted the designs to be very similar in style to the Reusch backhands. After this I went with Sondico, Mitre, Umbro and HO, and had input into all the designs/cuts. The best pair were the Umbros I wore around 2009/10 time."

I've still kept to this day. I've always been a hoarder!"

David's pair of Reusch World Cup 90s were in the early range of roll finger gloves pioneered by USA keeper Tony Meola: "They were given to me by Tony himself when he came over from America and

69

PANINI KEEPERS

Starting with a news stand in Modena in 1945, two of the four Panini brothers (Benito and Giuseppe) expanded to a newspaper distribution office in the 1950s before venturing into the collectables market with siblings Franco and Umberto. Beginning with images of plants and flowers, a set of football cards then proved even more popular. Panini were not the first manufacturer to hatch the idea of

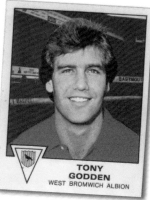

TONY GODDEN
WEST BROMWICH ALBION

ABERDEEN

BOBBY CLARK

WOLVERHAMPTON

GARY PIERCE

housing their cards in a collectable album, but they quickly became the leader of the pack.

Numerically, Zaccaria Cometti of Atalanta was the first goalkeeper to appear in a Panini album, *Calciatori 1961-62*. His card – as they were at the time rather than self-adhesive stickers – was number four in the first album covering the Italian domestic league.

Among the famous goalkeepers to feature in the album was Lorenzo Buffon, of Inter, a cousin of the grandfather of Gian-luigi Buffon – a latter-day stopper who ranks highly among the most Panini appearances.

Panini's first foray into distribution outside Italy coincided with the 1970 World Cup. *Mexico 70* was available in three versions – Italian, English and International – presented as a mixture of stickers and, primarily, cards.

Card number 13 was lucky for those with a goalkeeping fetish as two legends of the 1930s appeared – Gianpiero Combi and František Plánička, shaking hands before the 1934 World Cup Final between Italy and Czechoslovakia.

Among the regular teams in Panini's World Cup debut was 1966 World Cup winner Gordon Banks, West Germany's Sepp Maier and Italy's Dino Zoff – who would go on to be a veteran of four such albums, culminating

BRIGHTON & HOVE A.
GRAHAM MOSELEY

WEST HAM UNITED
PHIL PARKES

TOTTENHAM
RAY CLEMENCE

HANS VAN BREUKELEN
NOTTINGHAM FOREST

STEVE SHERWOOD
WATFORD

1976-77 season, Panini simultaneously entered the UK market under their own moniker with *Euro Football*. At the time, FKS had been dominating the English football sticker (or picture stamp) market; but a sea change occurred when Panini gave away 250,000 *Euro Football* albums with *Shoot!* magazine.

The self-adhesive backs made for a much easier collecting process, and the series also captured the imagination as it opened a window to the exotic world of football outside of the UK. Poland's Jan Tomaszewski brought back bad memories to many England fans while Ivo Viktor took his place in the album fresh from starring in goal for Czechoslovakia in their 1976 European Championship victory.

MARTIN THOMAS

with his triumphant appearance in *Espana 82*.

Intent on achieving world domination in the sticker market, Panini's first domestic football album outside of Italy came with *Football 1972-73* in Belgium.

By this point, Panini was also moving tentatively into the English football market by collaborating with London publishers Top Sellers who produced the First Division albums *Football 72* to *Football 77*.

Starting out as cards, by the end of its run the Top Sellers/Panini fusion was totally made up of stickers representing the English game's finest. Pat Jennings enjoyed the distinction of featuring on the album cover and sticker packet for both *Football 74* and *Football 77*, having been named as Footballer of the Year in 1973 and 1976.

While continuing to fulfil their duty with Top Sellers during the

Boosted by the huge success of *Euro Football,* Panini brought out a first album, under their own name, dedicated to English and Scottish football.

Again given away free with *Shoot!*, *Football 78* was the start of the brand's golden era in the UK.

Fittingly, Pat Jennings – now having moved to Arsenal from Tottenham – was the first goalkeeper to appear in *Football 78*, along with a Who's Who of 1970s goalkeeping royalty:

TONY COTON
WATFORD

STEVE OGRIZOVIC
COVENTRY CITY

Panini beat Movember to the punch, with some fine 'taches on display.

71

HENRY SMITH

CHRIS TURNER

images until David Seaman had the opening shot all to himself for *Football 92*.

Robert Maxwell's takeover of the company during the summer of 1988 precipitated the beginning of the end for Panini's domination of the UK collectables market.

However, the previous output up to *Football 88* continues to hold adults in thrall of a bygone era, when they were swapping their way towards the holy grail of a completed album.

Shilton, Clemence, Montgomery, Bonetti, Stepney, Rough…

Clemence was the first goalie to appear on the front of Panini's UK domestic football range, one of five images on the cover of *Football 78*. But after Danish goalkeeper Birger Jensen made a sneak cover appearance

Having lost out on the Premier League collectables licence to Merlin when it first became available for the 1993-94 season, much excitement was generated among veteran collectors when Panini finally won the right to produce the 2019-20 sticker album.

As Panini approaches their 60th anniversary, global interest in football stickers – both old and new – shows no sign of diminishing.

With thanks to Greg Lansdowne, author of Stuck On You, the definitive story of Panini.

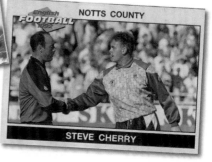

ALEC CHAMBERLAIN

STEVE CHERRY

in *Football 79* – playing for Club Brugge against Liverpool in the European Cup final – outfield skirmishes held sway as lead cover

RON SPRINGETT LAUDER MILLAR LYMPETS

"Wet or dry, muddy or clean, the ball is always hard to hold. Any goalie who has ever let a catch slip through his fingers will will be glad to know that, at last, help is literally to hand..."

Invented in 1955 by Charles Longworth Scholes and patented in 1955, Ron Springett's 'Lympet' goalkeeping gloves by Lauder Millar were a benchmark, seeing an English keeper's name first association with a pair of mitts.

asking for his autograph in 1966 and was sent the promotional leaflet by return – but sadly no autograph!

It's fascinating to find out more of the story behind these landmark gloves, long familiar only from the adverts carried in *Charles Buchan's Football Monthly*.

It turns out that Lauder Millar, "experts and leaders in the field of specialist glove manufacture," tweaked the design of their existing driving gloves, whose 'Lympet' grippers had been developed to offer a positive, sensitive grip on the wheel.

Aware that they had "helped to solve another gripping problem in the world of sport," Lauder Millar were proud to boast that their World Cup-friendly gloves had been "tried and whole-heartedly approved at games far and wide."

Our thanks go out to Ian Nannestad, editor of the excellent *Soccer History* magazine, who sent us this great piece of advertising material. Ian wrote to the Sheffield Wednesday & England keeper

One of the Uxbridge Road's finest establishments for any budding cat.

BAGS AND GLOVEBAGS

Walking to school with your cool Pat
Jennings bag from Argos stuffed with books,
pencil case and packed lunch used to feel
special – just like walking out on to the pitch
with your glovebag full to bursting with
pairs of gloves, peaked cap, spare tie-ups
and lucky mascot...

Even if your mascot was never quite as
successful as Gordon Stewart's 'Fred the
Skeleton' in *Roy of the Rovers'* 'The Safest
Hands in Soccer'.

Looking back, I remember cramming all
my old gloves into my first Sukan Sports
glovebag, so I couldn't even do up the zipper.
None of the extra, worn-out gloves I was
carrying were ever going to get game time,
I just wanted to
look the part,
like all the top
keepers I studied so closely on TV.

The original, first ever Sukan Sports
glovebag wasn't exactly your standard
glovebag, of the type that became familiar in

later years. It was in fact an ordinary, off-the-shelf pencil case made by a company called Conquest Products, just up the road from where Dave Holmes ran his glove emporium in Caversham. But once it had been printed

Table Tennis

COVERS   C18
C17 Wallet
New wallet shaped bat
cover for the tournament
player
C18 Super Bat
Black P.V.C. cover with fitted
ball pocket.
C19 Super Bat
Black P.V.C. cover   C19
22

Sondico logo no-go: we prefer to think 'coiled snake', not 'SS'...

with the futuristic Sukan Sports logo, it seemed to take on a whole new magical air. The kind of kit that only a real goalkeeper would ever own.

Dave had the ingenious idea of producing it in bright yellow, so it could easily be spotted when the cameras focused on the goal area.

It was undoubtedly product placement of the highest order – right up there with Mr Sondhi's quick conversion job on an existing table-tennis 'wallet' for his celebrity endorsees, messrs Clemence and Shilton.

OUR signed pennant for the "Question of the Week" goes to 13-year-old **Monique Paternoster** of **'Cornerways', The Green, Grundisburgh,** who wants to ask goalkeeper Paul Cooper what he keeps in the bag he keeps in the goal at every game.

PAUL SAYS — The bag contains several items like a few pairs of gloves which I might wear depending on the conditions, some chewing gum, some elastic bands which help to keep the gloves in place, a cap to wear in case of strong sunshine and a lucky mascot which has been working quite well for me this season!

Sporting evolution: From pencil case to glovebag.

77

WILLIAMS

Alex Williams MBE is best remembered as the goalie who finally took the place of the great Joe Corrigan in the City side of the early '80s. But how did that feel? And did Joe take an interest in his deputy's development?

"It was a real honour to replace Joe Corrigan. When he left to play out in America, I felt the club would bring in a more exper-ienced keeper, but

ALEX WILLIAMS

I kept my place. At the end of my first season I was voted into the Second Division team of the season by all the players. Big Joe was very helpful when I played under him, and he was a great person for me to learn from. We've since become great friends and we still work together on matchdays as part of the former players meet-and-greet group."

Did you train together? And what did the sessions consist of?

"The training sessions back in the day were very physical. We often trained together with Steve Fleet who was the youth-team coach at the time and a former Manchester City keeper, understudy to the great Bert Trautmann. When I got into the first team it was Alan Hodgkinson, the former Sheffield United and England keeper."

Making your debut as a fan of Manchester City, what was that experience like?

"The day went very quickly, I was told to report to Maine Road, and be ready to play if needed. The game was against West Brom, and John Bond gave me the shout an hour before. I was very proud to play, the first black goalkeeper of the modern era. West Brom's away colours were green and yellow stripes so I played in a bright red goalkeeper's shirt. I couldn't have been more colourful. I remember early in the game tipping a header over the bar, which settled the nerves. We won the game 2-1. Bryan Robson scored a late consolation for WBA; he also scored against me in my last game for City, while playing for United."

In that horrible '80s period of racism from the terraces, how did you cope?

"I never thought of myself as a black keeper, just a keeper. When I received stick from the fans it made me try harder. One of my best games was at West Ham, we got beat 5-0 but I was named Man of the Match as it should have been ten. In the first minute I saved a Ray Stewart penalty. I think, at the time, he had the hardest shot in football, and he had never missed one. After the game the West Ham fans made a guard of honour for me and clapped me off the pitch."

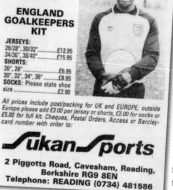

Alex's photo in the Sukan ad came from an official Umbro/England photoshoot to launch the new kit.

Who were the three best keepers you've ever seen play?

"Pat Jennings was my goalkeeping hero, plus Peter Shilton and Ray Clemence. A special mention must go to big Joe Corrigan."

What were your first pair of proper latex-palmed gloves, and can you remember how you came to get hold of them?

"I can't honestly remember what my first pair of synthetic gloves were. I think they were from Sukan Sports and made by Uhlsport, but I changed shortly after to Umbro, our kit sponsors. Of all the gloves I wore, I did like the Uhlsport. They fitted well and had great grip. I think I got free gloves from Uhlsport, but no money!"

Lastly, do you recall becoming a model for Sukan Sports' new Umbro GK kit ad?

"At that time I was in the 1984 England Under-21 squad. There was myself, Sammy Lee and Steve McMahon. We travelled down together in a car, it was a great day out. We were the last England side to win the European Championship at that level."

MY GOALKEEPING HERO

Neville Southall | Pat Jennings & Phil Parkes

"Pat Jennings was my idol but Phil Parkes did something special for me when I'd just got into the Everton team by sorting me out some gloves from his shop, Sukan Sports. He went out of his way for me, which I will never forget. A perfect gentlemen."

79

SCHOOL'S OUT FOR SUMMER

In the non-stop memories 'n' memorabilia-fest loosely known as the lives of us *Glove Story 2* authors, there's little room for the regret which lurks at the bitter end of the bittersweet nostalgic experience. A cheerfully course details lovingly preserved from back in the day, we're all feeling

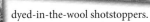

that we might have missed out on a fantastic working holiday that would have built character while providing even more idyllic memories to exaggerate. And two of us aren't even born-and-bred,

shallow bunch, we habitually accentuate the positives of the rose-tinted past... except perhaps where Bob Wilson Goalkeeping Schools are concerned.

Having long studied the adverts, the feedback from youthful attendees, the photos and now Bob's very own folder of top tips, timetables and

dyed-in-the-wool shotstoppers. Ahhh, what might have been. It breaks us up a little bit, just imagining the thrill of waking up for seven consecutive mornings in a stately home, getting to share Big Joe Corrigan's giant fry-up breakfast, and then flying into mud for hours on end.

The BWGS plays on our minds

THURSDAY

8.00 - 8.45	Breakfast
8.55 - 9.15	Video Work
9.30 - 12.00	Field - Pressure Work
	The whole morning will be devoted to working under pressure emphasising fitness, never surrendering.
	Exercises to include
	1. Piggy in the Middle
	2. Triangles
	3. Close range reactions
	4. Saving with feet
	5. Diving at feet - grids
	6. Continuous barrage a) servers
	b) balls laid into target & shot
	7. Corrigan session
	The break will be taken as normal is approx 10.30 unless we are all KNACKERED
12.30 - 1.30	Lunch
2.00 - 4.00	The Final Circuit - to refresh all remind
	1. Deflections
	2. Turn & Face
	3. Move & Save
	4. 1 v 1
	5. Long distance shots
	6. Saving with feet/legs etc
4.00 - 5.00	Shower & final pack
5.00 - 5.30	Presentation & Award Ceremony
5.30	Time for a well deserved drink, kip, sauna etc !

like the perfect amalgam of a dream school trip, a delightful Army boot camp of the type favoured by Goldie Hawn and the best game we ever played between the sticks.

Of all Bob's archive material, our hearts were most wrenched by a report in a youth side's newsletter, written by a parent from the Isle of Wight who joined his sons for a week of keeping goal. He made new friends. He suffered adverse weather and three minor injuries. He got to play five-a-side with Gary Mabbutt. And eventually he came to appreciate the unique role of the goalkeeper as outsider, as last line of defence, as anti-goalscorer and team within a team...

"I will finish with Bob's own words, loosely quoted. 'A goalkeeper's skills, techniques, problems and training are rarely understood or acknowledged by either his own team-mates, his manager or other club officials.' He is right, but I for one now have more understanding."

192 square feet. A massive, bloody great chasm!

81

GLOVE BRAND: ADIDAS

From the era of Ivan Curkovic to Toni Schumacher through to that of Edwin van der Sar and then Manuel Neuer, Adidas gloves have continually been evolving, year after year. Starting out with a simple trefoil stitched into woollen gloves, designs now go as far as to colour co-ordinate with the jerseys and boots you're wearing.

Adidas were one of the first glove manufacturers to be seen on the hands of keepers here in England. The distinctive black/white model endorsed by Saint Etienne's Ivan Curkovic was a huge step forward from bare hands or thin cotton gloves, sported by the likes of Ray Clemence and Peter Shilton prior to them signing with Sondico Sports; also by John Burridge, Jim Blyth and Pat Jennings, to name just a few.

As Pat Jennings confirmed in conversation, many keepers who were contracted to wear Adidas boots were given the Curkovic gloves to try by the Adidas rep.

Trying to purchase Adidas gloves and jerseys in the '80s wasn't always easy for us junior shotstoppers, and even Sukan Sports struggled at times to get sufficient stock to satisfy customers' orders. Luckily, living in Portsmouth – which just happened to be twinned with Duisburg – we often played tournaments in Germany as schoolboys. This gave me the chance to pore over the glove displays in local sports shops, which were seemingly designed to taunt us English cats, showing us what we were missing out on!

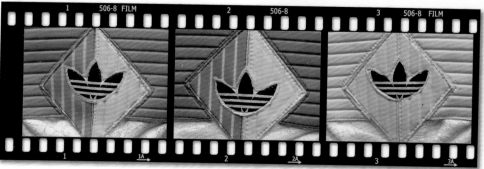

Trefoils, Three Stripes and Fingersaves - gloves for every occasion.

Memorable GOALKEEPING No 5 MOMENTS

GORDON BANKS
N. IRELAND 0-1 ENGLAND
Date: 15 May 1971
Venue: Windsor Park

A partisan Belfast crowd of 40,000 cheered when George Best cheekily shadowed Gordon Banks as he prepared to launch a drop-kick. And they cheered yet louder when their hero snaked out his left boot and toed the ball – just as it was floating in mid air for a fraction of a second – over the keeper and headed it into the empty net. But Scottish referee Alistair MacKenzie spoiled the fun, heeding Banks's protests and controversially disallowing the goal.

Even future England captain Emlyn Hughes, present that day, admitted it should have stood. "Without a shadow of doubt, it was a goal," he declared. "Banks bounced the ball a couple of times and George was watching him. Suddenly he nipped in and chipped the ball with his toe and before Gordon could look round it was in the net. It was an act of perfect timing, a sporting piece of genius. The referee was out of order. It was an injustice that the goal was disallowed."

RAY CLEMENCE'S FAMOUS WORLD CUP APPEARANCE

Okay, so it was just in a computer game rather than under searing sun in an exotic cauldron of sporting legend. But at least Ray emerged with great credit. Right?

Released by Macmillan Software in 1986, just in time for Mexico, World Cup Soccer looked like a winner for any schoolkid with a ZX Spectrum and an unusually fervent imagination.

Ray introduced the game as a must for any serious and dedicated soccer fan; but, well... he never was exactly shy when it came to endorsing a whole grab-bag of random products.

According to our old mate Chris Oakley's Football Attic Videoblog, "It's a strange kind of a game in that it contains a database of information on previous World Cups. All harmless fun," Chris reckons, and he should know 'cos he

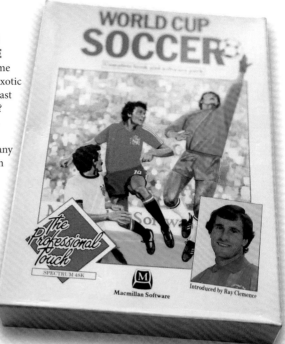

Virtual Ray (left) and real Ray (above). Hard to tell apart, like World Cup Soccer vs. real life.

at half-time. Then the real fun starts: there's a tricky heading challenge (see screenshot) and a Pong-style shooting game to determine the winner... and ultimately it's Ray himself, who probably made £30 for his thumbs-up!

With thanks to Chris Oakley, now proprietor at kitbliss.co.nz.

had this long-lost game as a thrill-seeking 14 year old. "But then you turned the cassette over and loaded side two for a bit more in the way of entertainment. Here was the game aspect of World Cup Soccer..."

Chris picks his England side, rather bafflingly from a list of global greats. The game chooses groups and fixtures, does a bit of automatic calculating and suddenly it's England 1-1 Hungary

85

MATCHWORN MEMORIES

The roar of the liniment, the smell of the crowd... nothing beats the authenticity of an item of vintage goalkeeping memorabilia that was actually centre-stage at a big match, worn by one of your goalkeeping favourites.

First up is a Celtic corker worn by Packie Bonner in Danny McGrain's testimonial game. On 4th August 1980, the Hoops took on Manchester United – and

night he saved the match-winning penalty in the 1983/84 UEFA Cup final. Parks kept his shirt and later gave it to his son, Joe. Tragically, Joe died in 2015 and Parks loaned the shirt for inclusion in his memory. From the same book, we're also thrilled to see Ray

here's hoping not too many of the Parkhead crowd noticed the spelling error on the back of the Irish goalie's jersey! Thanks to Paul Lamb for sharing this ultra rarity.

Next come two superb exhibits from Simon Shakeshaft, Daren Burney & Neville Evans, authors of *The Spurs Shirt Book*. Tony Parks' shirt dates from the

Clemence's rare red match shirt from the 1986/87 season.

Thanks to Dave Hitchman, we have below Nigel Spinks' Aston Villa jerseys from the early '90s, while above are two memorable Derby County shirts courtesy of Phil Lowe.

The Le Coq Sportif was matchworn by David McKeller in 1979/80. Steve Cherry's Patrick dates back to the 1983/84 FA Cup tie v Plymouth Argyle where he let one in from a

corner. It was never to be worn again!

Thanks to Simon Shakeshaft & James Elkin, authors of *The Arsenal Shirt*, for John Lukic's Adidas shirt from 1986-89 and for Pat

Jennings' Umbro, matchworn circa 1979.

Rob O'Donnell kindly provided Ian Andrews' Leicester City 1985-86 bobby dazzler above, while Mark McCarthy loaned his 1984-86 Manchester City shirt,

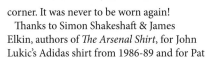

matchworn by Alex Williams, Eric Nixon and Barry Siddall.

David Sproat recently generously returned his Newcastle United 1985/86 shirt to its original owner, Martin Thomas, who gave it away back in the day. Note the Reusch transfer, neatly ironed on by Martin's wife!

The Everton Le Coq Sportif shirt was worn by Neville Southall for the famous save he made from Mark Falco at White Hart Lane. Thanks to Sam @bluetoffee9. And finally to Steve Plant for the jerseys of Mark Kendall. A genuine Uhlsport with embroidered badge logo; and who knows when the Wolves GK wore this yellow Spall shirt – not at home, nor away when the opposition clashed with Wolves' old gold?!?

The days when Uhlsport jerseys could be worn under the radar of the club's main kit manufacturer.

Legends on the line No 6 Alan Knight

Alan 'The Legend' Knight holds the goalkeeper's appearance record for a single club with a total of 801 games for Portsmouth from 1978 to 2000...

You made your League debut at Rotherham, aged 16. What sort of gloves did you use as a youngster?

"I used gardening gloves that were orange and had a criss-cross pattern on the palm, and were absolute useless, especially when it started raining. Then along came the green cotton Peter Bonetti ones, also the table-tennis style he brought out that had the

SPORTS MAIL

POMPEY MUST THANK KNIGHT

Preston stalemate

pimples on the palm. Again, useless. Only good to keep your hands warm on a cold day. Gloves have come a long way since the '70s; but at the time, whether it was bare hands or cotton gloves, it taught you the art of catching a ball properly in all conditions."

How did you become aware of the new latex gloves a few years later?

"Through Peter Mellor, as we were sponsored by Gola at the time and they had given him some pairs to use. To be honest, they were pretty basic and had a thin palm but were a massive step up from the green cotton Bonettis. Then I moved on to a pair of Adidas (Curkovic) that were black with a white pimpled palm. I normally had to buy my own or go cap in hand to the club and ask them to buy me some pairs. Later on, when I was established in the team, I was supplied gloves free of charge by Dave at Sukan Sports, and this varied from Uhlsport to Reusch plus the ones like Sepp Maier that had the 'S' on the backhand."

When you broke into the senior ranks at Portsmouth did you get any specialist coaching?

"At the end of the morning, Peter Mellor and I would get together with manager Frank Burrows and go through handling and crosses. This was mixed in with

90

was my least favourite. In one game I suffered a bad injury when Eric Young left his mark on me – and a terrible Noel Blake own-goal. We always knew we were in for a battle when we went there. Good against evil in football terms. Fair play to Bally [Pompey boss Alan Ball], he soon got my confidence back and had me diving at people's feet in training as soon as the face had healed up; though he didn't manage to get me coming for crosses again!"

You once experienced a glovebag and its contents being stolen from the net...

"It was away at Huddersfield. At the end of the game it had gone! Someone had jumped over the barrier and helped himself. If he could send it back via the club, I'll stick them on eBay – must be worth something now!"

five-a-side games and shooting drills but we didn't have any real specialist coaching, we just worked each other. A bit later on, Mike Kelly would come in a couple of times a week, while working freelance for other clubs. He was one of the first breed of goalkeeper coaches and he was a right taskmaster. He absolutely killed me in sessions."

You sometimes used Uhlsport or Reusch jerseys in matches, rather than those of the club's official suppliers...

"I didn't get much say in the styles or colours, as you could probably tell by some of the shockers I was given to wear. The Uhlsport jerseys came about because the Admiral one I was given in that season we had in Division One was awful, it was yellow and had black flappy collars which was like one of my old school shirts. I'm sure you can find a photo somewhere!"

You played in all four divisions and at a large number of grounds. Apart from Fratton Park, did you have any favourites?

"I would have to say Boundary Park, Oldham. Not the most glamorous of grounds but I always seem to have a good game when we played there. Plough Lane, Wimbledon

MY GOALKEEPING HERO

Tony Coton | Pat Jennings

"What I really admired about him was the way he could take crosses with one hand. I only have two autographs in pride of place in my study. One is Muhammad Ali and the other is big Pat's. I was on a coaching course with him some years ago and I got him to sign an old Spurs goalkeeper's shirt for me. A real gentlemen of the game."

BRUCE FORSYTH'S BIG NIGHT – AND DAVE'S TOO!

Brucie's *Big Night* was designed to be the Saturday night TV smash of 1978, the follow-up to *The Generation Game* after ITV cheekily poached Forsyth from Auntie Beeb.

In reality, Bruce's old show fared far better, even under the stewardship of Larry Grayson. For younger readers, think *Ant & Dec's Saturday Night Takeaway*; older readers, seriously consider why you weren't down the pub.

The show featured audience-participation games such as 'Beat The Goalie', where viewers phoned in and aimed a penalty, a bit like *The Golden Shot*. Among the guest keepers that appeared were Pat Jennings, Phil Parkes, Jimmy Rimmer, Kevin Keelan, Peter

Bonetti, Alex Stepney, Ray Clemence, Tony Godden and Gary Bailey.

One lucky 15 year old from Portsmouth, Dave Bowers, got the opportunity of a lifetime to appear on the show. After entering a competition in the *TV Times* he was selected to be phoned by Bruce to guide a

ball past the current Liverpool & England goalkeeper, Ray Clemence. And he was successfully in doing so, in a time of 4.48 seconds, which earned him £50 and a trip to London, along with his parents, to appear on the show the following week.

"It was brilliant," Dave told us. "They paid for us to come up to London from Portsmouth and put us up in a posh hotel, all expenses paid. Bruce was great, and they treated us so well, we even had Jimmy Rimmer make us all a cup of coffee in the green room before the show".

Decked out coolly in his leather jacket and fetching blue roll-neck, Dave took to the specially built ball machine and proceeded to fire two goals past the boxing legend John Conteh in his boxing gloves – earning himself an opportunity to go for a further

prize. With irresistible booty such as a typewriter and fishing tackle up from grabs, Dave had his heart set on the billiard table. But after three hits he came away with a projector and screen. "After the show, Bruce

came and saw us and actually offered me the billiard table," Dave revealed. "But my dad intervened and said it wouldn't fit in the house. My dad then went on to give me £50

TONY GODDEN'S BIG NIGHT

Tony Godden made a guest appearance on Bruce Forsyth's *Big Night* recently as the star goalkeeper in their penalty prize competition.

Played something on the *Golden Shot* basis where the contestants direct the shot by giving instructions to the competitors, Tony had very little knowledge of where the shot would go until it had been fired because of the studio lights.

Said Tony: "It was a tremendous experience. Everyone connected with the show was very helpful and kind."

"During the show I met disc jockey Ed Stewart and he was saying he was disappointed, he could not make the match at Goodison as he is an Everton fan. As it was, the match was called off."

for the projector and screen". Ever realised, 40 years after the event, that you were done up like a kipper, folks? And yet there was still another twist to Dave's foray into nationwide

TV stardom. The following week, a letter came through the door addressed to Dave... "It was from John Deacon, the Portsmouth chairman. He'd seen the show and noted

that I was a big Pompey fan. Enclosed was a season ticket for the rest of the season for the South Stand. This was a great gesture, but I did have to write back and ask for one for the North Stand instead, so I could be with my mates as this is where we always stood".

Hats off!: Absolute respect to Phil, his dreamy golden locks and the wonders of Cossack gentlemen's firm-hold.

TIP-TOP TIPS

No matter whether you're a young goalie, a parks goalie, a pro goalie or an cx goalie, it's never too late to learn. All set? Yes, coach!

Anglo Confectionery's *Football Hints* is often considered the bible of hot tips, a 12-volume set of booklets prepared with the co-operation of the Football Association. Straight from the horse's mouth, see? And lots of the exact same tips also appeared on the back of Anglo's World Cup 70 football cards, so they must have been good.

Volume 1, *Goalkeeping Hints*, featured Bonetti on trigonometry, Banks on diving and Shilton on fanciful hairstyles for the coming decade. Drink in these tips and put them into action today.

In the era of the sweeper keeper, there's lots more for goalies to learn from the outfield booklets, too. Ignore at your peril the contents of *Heading, Ball Control* and *Special Kicks* (dummy, overhead and scissor (2020 Health & Safety advisory: do not attempt while running).

JUMP TO IT

IN wet weather even the softest shot aimed above your head should never be caught with your feet on the ground. A miss-handle will lead to the ball dropping behind your head over the line. Always jump up and catch the ball in your chest because even if the ball escapes from your grasp it is trapped in your rib cage.

Into the '80s, Sobinerry produced a set of vital Goalkeeping Skillcards featuring Paul Cooper of Ipswich Town.

Touted in *Match Weekly* as "a unique set of 10 cards specially designed to help you as a young goalkeeper develop your potential," they're still great for anyone "who wants to learn the techniques that may some day make them into a professional."

It was great to learn how to deal with crosses and corners – also how to deal from the bottom of the pack so that your mates got all the cards that involved any possibility

94

BRICK WALL

IN wet weather never simply bend from the waist for the low shot driven directly at you. If the wet ball escapes from your grasp it's odds-on a goal. Go down on one knee and, with your legs forming an additional wall, collect the ball and hug it to your chest.

of danger. Here's a nice easy one for you: Simply stand in the bathroom in your full goalie kit and arrange two mirrors so that it is possible to see the back of your head. Not only recommended for checking out bald spots, this technique also gives you a useful insight into how it looks to opposition

Most goalkeepers find the high cross ball difficult to deal with, which is surprising when you think that the goalkeeper has the advantage of being able to use his hands. Peter Bonetti is extremely good at "taking" high balls. He makes certain that his hands always provide a barrier to the ball and the fingers are spread out. Most important of all, watch the ball.

NARROWING THE ANGLE.
The goalkeeper is at his most vulnerable on his goal line. That is when the forwards can see most of the goal. As the goalkeeper comes out from his goal so the space into which a forward can shoot decreases.

A goalkeeper should come out from his goal when the last line of his defence is beaten.

He must then move quickly, but under control so that he can dive or jump to save shots. If he has to dive at the opponent's feet he must present a long barrier to his goal with his body.

All good goalkeepers have quick reactions and few have quicker reactions than Peter Shilton of Leicester City. Diving to save shots requires quick reactions. The goalkeeper who is quick dives in time to get his body behind the ball. The goalkeeper who is slow dives as the ball is passing him — at least he dives on top of the ball — but the ball can very easily skid out of the goalkeeper's grip. Goalkeepers remember — Get the body behind the ball — avoid exposing the ball to the opponent's boot as illustrated below.

Artist's impression: A '60s Shilton snap kindly restyled to reflect the dawn of the '70s.

forwards when you're picking the ball out of the net.

Do it often enough, and you can work up a deep-seated, pathological hatred of conceding which will stand you in good stead for the long winter ahead.

And so to this smashing old Mitre poster crammed with multiple 'Goalkeeping Tips with Bob Wilson'.

We'll end today's session with Bob's ultimate, toppermost tip. "Good, confident handling by keepers requires all kinds of attributes but the most important basic requirement is strong forearms, wrists, palms and fingers. A good exercise to develop these is to simply squeeze a tennis ball in any spare time. Do it whenever watching TV."

Better still, do it when reading *Glove Story 2* – and for best effect don't stop until the arrival of *Glove Story 3!*

95

Memorable GOALKEEPING No 6 MOMENTS

JIMMY GLASS
Carlisle United 2-1 Plymouth Argyle
Date: 8th May 1999, 4.55pm
Venue: Brunton Park

It's the final day of the season, and Carlisle United need a win to remain in the Football League. The score is tied at one apiece with seconds remaining. Then Carlisle get a corner-kick. Jimmy Glass, the keeper on loan from Swindon Town, looks across at his manager Nigel Pearson, who waves him forward. With his red-and-black Eddie Stobart-sponsored shirt and Uhlsport gloves, Glass makes his late run into the box.

Graham Anthony swings in the corner which is met by Scott Dobie. His header is saved by the Plymouth keeper James Dungey; but it's only parried out to where the advancing Glass has ghosted in. He meets it first time... and his shot hits the net.

Ecstatic, incredulous fans descend from the stands to celebrate with their team. Even the referee is hugged to the ground.

If only Barrie Tomlinson had thought of this plot for *Roy of the Rovers,* it would have been a Charlie Carter story long before 1999.

And here comes Jimmy Glass...

ALVIN MARTIN'S HAT-TRICK – AGAINST THREE DIFFERENT GKs

A quiz question for you. Which England international scored a hat-trick against three different keepers in the same match?

Martin Thomas knows the answer as he was the starting goalkeeper for Newcastle United on that day back in 1986.

"Dave McKellar and Gary Kelly were the goalkeepers at the time, as I'd been out for six months and had just started my rehab. Manager Willie McFaul invited me to travel with the team for Chelsea on the Saturday and West Ham on the Monday.

We arrived at the training ground on the Friday morning; Gary Kelly plays head tennis in the gym, does his knee ligaments and is out for the season!

"So Dave McKeller has to play v Chelsea; but he then ruptures his groin late in the

other than some basic handling so I said I would play. I then go and dislocate the same shoulder early in the game and have to go off. Chris Hedworth then went in goal and he

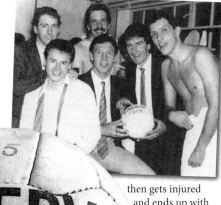

The day when Upton Park witnessed Alvin's one and only, very special hat-trick.

then gets injured and ends up with a broken collar bone.

"Then Peter Beardsley donned the gloves and went in goal for the remainder of the game!"

In the interest of balance, we simply had to ask Alvin Martin about the incident: "It was the only hat-trick of my career," he beamed.

game and is out for the season!

"The club apply for an emergency loan to cover, but it's after the Football League deadline. Willie asked me if I felt all right to play as we had no other options in goal except outfield players. I'd been back about a week and done no goalkeeping

"I'd already scored a couple when we were awarded a penalty. We were 7-1 up at the time, and the crowd were chanting my name to take it.

"Ray Stewart was our usual penalty taker so I pulled rank as captain and stepped up to complete my only ever hat-trick past Peter Beardsley – who, ironically, I roomed with out in Mexico for the World Cup that summer!"

We wondered if Alvin still has the ball?

"Give me a few minutes and I'll send you a photo," he replied. What a legend!

WEST HAM UNITED

1 PHIL PARKES
2 RAY STEWART
3 GEORGE PARRIS
4 TONY GALE
5 ALVIN MARTIN (capt.)
6 ALAN DEVONSHIRE
7 MARK WARD
8 MARK McAVENNIE
9 ALAN DICKENS
10 TONY COTTEE
11 NEILL ORR
12

NEWCASTLE UNITED

1 MARTIN THOMAS
2 NEIL McDONALD
3 JOHN BAILEY
4 DAVID McCREERY
5 JEFF CLARKE
6 GLENN ROEDER (capt.)
7 PAUL STEPHENSON
8 JOHN ANDERSON
9 BILLY WHITEHURST
10 PETER BEARDSLEY
11 TONY CUNNINGHAM
12

97

GLOVE BRAND: SELLS

Going strong since the final day of 2001, when Adam Sells' glove brand first burst on to the scene, Sells Goalkeeper Products have graced the hands of countless fine keepers all over the world.

Like many glove obsessives, Adam was a regular customer of Sukan Sports in his teenage years, and progressed from wearing many different brands to manufacturing his own.

From the Valley in

the cup in a pair of Sells gloves. He thought Adam was bonkers. But when he did finally hoist high the trophy in the Ataturk Stadium,

he thought of Adam because his dream had actually come true.

We naturally assume that

Charlton, where Dean Kiely was Sells' first endorsee, the brand grew quickly to an early highlight in Istanbul in 2005 when Liverpool's Jerzy Dudek performed heroics against AC Milan, coming back from 3-0 down to win the UEFA Champions League trophy.

In Dudek's autobiography, *A Big Pole in Our Goal*, he reveals that Adam told him of a premonition he'd had during the group stages of the – that Jerzy would go on to the lift

producing gloves is a glamorous life, and every day is being spent diving around, testing out the latest gloves with

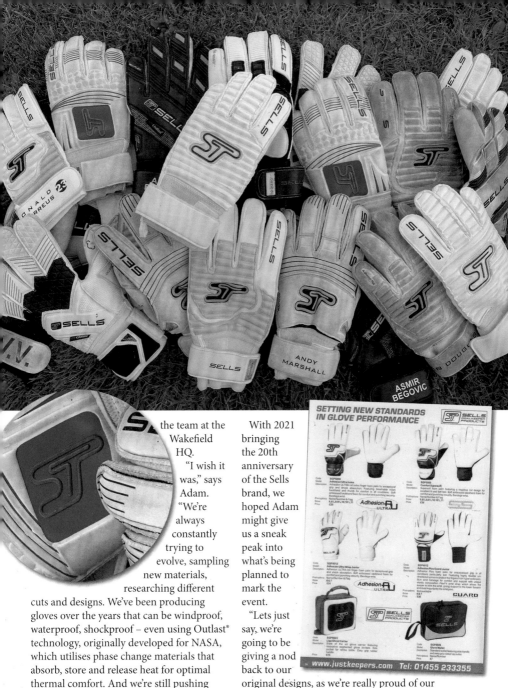

the team at the Wakefield HQ.

"I wish it was," says Adam. "We're always constantly trying to evolve, sampling new materials, researching different cuts and designs. We've been producing gloves over the years that can be windproof, waterproof, shockproof – even using Outlast® technology, originally developed for NASA, which utilises phase change materials that absorb, store and release heat for optimal thermal comfort. And we're still pushing boundaries every year to find the highest quality parts for our keepers."

With 2021 bringing the 20th anniversary of the Sells brand, we hoped Adam might give us a sneak peak into what's being planned to mark the event.

"Lets just say, we're going to be giving a nod back to our original designs, as we're really proud of our heritage and the many gloves we've produced over the years".

JUMPERS FOR GOALPOSTS or THE GOALKEEPER COMPLEX

Take a group of eleven small children with a football and drop them in a park, in a playground or side street. Immediately, two trees or two drainpipes roughly the right distance apart become a goal. In the middle of a playing field or a stretch of desert with no discernible features, outer layers of clothing are soon instinctively stripped off for a higher purpose.

Ten of the kids proceed to gang up and smash the ball repeatedly toward the improvised goal. Just one of the kids takes

"Take your coat love, you'll need it."

Remember the first time you ever stood in a real, full-size goal, with an actual net?

"nice soft grass nice soft grass nice soft grass"

UMBRO
Only Football

sides with the parkas and does their best to protect the void between them. To prevent their schoolmates scoring and celebrating. To retain the integrity of the goal, and the precious status quo of the 0-0 scoreline.

The kid in goal is a natural custodian – the minder or guardian of the goal – and surely that's an overwhelmingly conservative state of mind.

But then the kid in goal is unafraid to be different and pick up the ball. It takes courage to step away from doing what everyone else is doing, and to try and stop them achieving the object of their game.

No one else is wearing gloves or a dirty peaked cap. Everyone else in the school team wears the same uniform, not some luminous, eye-boggling fancy-dress that looks like it's been designed by a three year old with a set of marker pens. And only one is carrying around a bagful of chewing-gum wrappers, water bottles and lucky charms.

The kid will never know the glory of scoring, but routinely faces the risk of danger and injury in the knowledge that any goal against will automatically be their fault.

The keeper is a reckless extrovert, a cautious outsider, a spoilsport acrobat masochist with a Maradona Complex.

And big gloves.

UMBRO
Only Football

101

SAVES GALORE!

Back in the '80s and '90s, *Saves Galore* was the video compilation series that kept us goalies going back time and time again.

By frantically fast-forwarding, playing and rewinding, we'd actually wear out the odd bit of tape where Neville Southall tipped a thunderbolt over the bar – in the same way other video enthusiasts got a grainy passage

sized plastic box. The stuff of every bloke's pre-digital dreams.

Once we had our gloved hands on the tape, all we had to do was wait for the TV and

RAY CLEMENCE

video player to come free so we could spend the 60 minutes in heaven, watching our goalkeeping heroes perform heroics to keep the ball from entering that net.

SAVES GALORE
1991 1992
THE OFFICIAL FOOTBALL LEAGUE VIDEO

FOX VIDEO
THE VERY BEST SAVES FROM THE 1991/92 BARCLAYS DIVISION ONE LEAGUE CHAMPIONSHIP

Still, to this day, many old goalkeepers talk about the compilations and can remember many of the saves that were on the tapes.

when the lads are looking through the dorm window in *Animal House*. Or so I'm told by my weird non-goalie mates...

There was no YouTube back then for us 50-somethings to watch, so we had to make do with a glorious VHS cassette tape (that's 'Video Home System', history fans). In other words, a spool of analogue tape in a letter-

Neville Southall would be a regular performer, so much so that the early years would be more or less a Neville showcase of some of his greatest saves.

The tape would be broken down month by month, with Ray giving his expert opinion on the best saves of the period, and the odd comedy blooper.

Jim Rosenthal and Ray Clemence would discuss the season's saves surrounded by an array of screens, editing equipment and a purple curtain to enhance the viewer's experience.

It was quite a thrill to have a coffee with Jim to talk about the videos – and then he kindly put us in touch with Dave Wood and Tony Mills, who were the brains behind the

season for each of the *Saves Galore!* seasons?

Well, winner of '88/89 best was Neville Southall (Everton) from John Barnes.

Winner of the 89/90 season was Bruce Grobbelaar (Liverpool) from Brian McClair.

And winner of '90/91 was Jan Stejskal (QPR) – now there's a name from the past – from a Mark Hughes shot.

Scandalously, there were no winners chosen for '91/92 and '92/93 – probably because it looked like a fix when Neville kept on winning every save of the season!

Say no more, it's 'The Southall Show'.

operation, for more behind-the-scenes facts.

The *Saves Galore* series ran for three seasons, 1988/89 to 1991/92, and then changed its name to *Saves, Saves, Saves* when the Premier League was formed for the 1992/93 season.

Ray and Jim worked on the first two but from '90/91 were replaced with commentary and voiceovers from the likes of Matthew Lorenzo, Brian Moore and illustrious co.

But which saves were voted the best of the

MORE SUKAN SPORTS STORIES

Back in the '80s, the first week of August was always an exciting time for me, but not because I was thinking of packing suitcases for a trip to the Isle of Wight or one of those new package holidays to the Costa Blanca.

I'd be starting my paper round at 7.00am and then rushing home to wait keenly for the postman, on lookout in my parents' front bedroom, before having to leave for school at 8.25, the last possible moment.

The reason? The Sukan Sports catalogue would be arriving in the post any day. Also inside that envelope would be a hand-typed list of last year's stock with prices heavily discounted, and sometimes a colour promotional ad, teasing you with reductions while tempting with the new season's range.

What's it going to be? Another pair of Uhlsports from the new selection, or a transfer switch to Umbro, Reusch or Sondico?

Choosing a pair of new gloves was a tough decision-making exercise in itself, which wasn't helped when your parents said you couldn't go past the £14 mark. Heartbreaking, when you could see a pair of top-end Reusch Pfaff for just a few pounds more.

The disappointment was crushing when the postman walked past the house or posted nothing but bills, as bad as letting in a last-minute goal. Except now I only had 24 hours to wait instead of the customary seven days to get it out of my system and go again.

Fast forward 40 years and I'm sitting at a coffee table in Caversham, sharing this story with Dave Holmes, the owner of Sukan Sports. At last, he now realises how much the arrival of his catalogue meant to a young

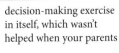

Mr. D. Holmes,   TE/BA
Sukan Sports,
St. Martin's Centre,
45 Church St.,
CAVERSHAM,
Reading,
Berkshire.   November 8, 1979

Dear Mr. Holmes,

Thank you for your letter dated November 6, 1979 booking a
½ page advertisement to appear in SHOOT Magazine issue dated
December 8, 1979.

This will be charged at £170.00. Would you kindly note that
this order is accepted on a pre-payment basis for which I confirm
receipt of your cheque for the sum of £170.00.

This order is accepted on the clear understanding that in
the event of an undue delay in supplying the goods requested by
readers, this delay will be advised. At the same time extending the
choice of awaiting goods ordered, a choice of alternative items or a
cash refund.

Yours sincerely,

pp. T. J Scrowey
T. Edinburgh
Advertisement Manager

with huge affection about every year in the business's 16-year lifespan.

I think the biggest shock for me was finding out that Dave's co-owner, Phil Parkes, never actually worked in the shop. I'd seen a brief TV feature on Sukan with Phil behind the counter, where he referred to a young Australian customer called Mark Bosnich who owed some money for a cap. Of course, this was just for the cameras. Mark, if you're reading this, you can relax. You don't owe any money, but we would love to know

cat in the '80s... though he does politely mention that he remembers me phoning (0734) 481586 persistently to ask if it had been sent out yet! Kids, eh? I wonder if my parents ever checked the phone bill and wondered who I knew in Reading?

Dave never fully realised the impact of Sukan Sports until he chanced across an internet forum where so many keepers of a certain age were reminiscing

if you still have the cap!

Over more recent years, I've been visiting Dave regularly at his home to talk about the Golden Age, drinking coffee for hours on end, leafing through old order books, catalogues and football programmes, listening to stories of pro keepers phoning up or popping in to get themselves fully kitted out for the season.

It was during just such a chat that I finally discovered where the shop's name originated.

"Sukan means 'sports' in Malay," Dave explained. "With my wife being Malaysian,

David James
31 Valley Rise
Garston, Watford
HERTS WD2 6EY

15th April 1987.

Dear Sukan Sports,
I am writing to you because I am looking for glove sponsorship. I am currently playing in the reserve side at Watford F.C. I am 16 years old and have been using Reusch gloves for the best part of the season, given to me by Tony Coton. I fmed the gloves much better to use than other brands, and I would really like to be sponsored by them.

yours
David James.

ADMIRAL SPORTSWEAR (UK) LTD.

SALES INVOICE

N? 5447
DATE 19.11.8
ORDER No.
DESPATCH NOTE No. 0

Sukan Sports
St Martins Precinct
5 Church St
Caversham
Reading

V.A.T. Reg. No. 200 3100 10

DUCT No.	DESCRIPTION	SIZE	QTY.	PRICE	TOTAL	V/
	England G/K Shirt	1	24	6.25	150.00	
		2	40	6.25	250.00	
		3	40	6.52	260.80	*
		4	30	6.52	195.60	*
		5	12	6.52	78.24	*
	Shorts	1	24	3.19	76.56	
		2	40	3.40	136.00	
		3	40	3.40	136.00	*
		4	30	3.59	107.70	*
		5	12	3.72	44.64	*
	Hose	Y	72	1.35	97.20	*
		M	72	1.35	97.20	*
					1629.94	
			VAT @ 15% on 966.51		144.97	
					1774.91	

INVOICE N? 11476
24 March 1981

Sukan Sports
St Martins Precinct
45 Church Street
CAVERSHAM-Reading Berks.

WEMBLEY STADIUM LIMITED
THE EMPIRE STADIUM, WEMBLEY, HA9 0DW

Cheques made payable to Wembley Stadium Limited, to be addressed to the Accountant.

V.A.T. No. 196 1174 56

Registered in England 223957

FOOTBALL LEAGUE CUP FINAL -14 March 1981.

Half page advert in the above programme	£200	00
+ Vat	30	00
	£230	00

UMBRO INTERNATIONAL LTD

you could say the name came from her.

"When Phil and myself started the business we wanted a name a bit different. Phil already had a couple of sports shops, 'Parksy's' and 'Phil Parkes Sports', so we needed to avoid using his name again.

"Starting out in 1979 we didn't have a lot of competition, given the cost of the gloves at the time. You have to remember, the cotton gloves from Metric and Sondico were less than £2 a pair so persuading goalkeepers to try a latex-palm glove for £12, which also wouldn't last long,

was something we had to consider. Meeting Gebhard Reusch at a German trade fair was a big contributing factor to our success in those early days.

"Obviously, having Phil's name behind us was also a great help, especially with his contacts in the game. We started the business above Stan Eldon Sports in Caversham then moved to a self-contained shop in Piggotts Road. Phil, with his carpentry skills, did a

lot of the work in getting it all done up. I'd started working in the sports trade in 1966, but virtually everyone I spoke to said a goalkeepers' goods mail-order company had little chance of working as a full-time job. I'll be forever grateful to Phil. I'm certain that if I'd tried to do it on my own it would never have been as successful as it turned out."

106

MIND THE GAP!

The first time we came across the strangely archaic topic of 'gapping' was in a late '60s football equipment catalogue from Elsey's, the Tottenham-based mail-order outfit. Concerned that we'd stumbled across some kind of obscure, somewhat shameful practice in this grubby pamphlet, our worst fears were hardly allayed by the accompanying caveat beneath

an illustration of sumptuously quilted goalkeeper's sweaters. Yes, you guessed, apparently it's only us goalies who need to worry about 'gapping'.

"Extra length," the garment's small-print description ran, "to ensure no 'gapping' when reaching for the high one."

Immediately, a creeping self-consciousness began to kick in.

Had we been 'gapping' for years, while not even close friends or team-mates had mustered the courage to address the issue? Were other players laughing behind our backs as our shirts rode up during an energetic save, exposing our non-designer Y-fronts or belly button?

How strange that, back in the '60s, '70s and '80s, it was considered something of a problem for a goalkeeper's jersey to momentarily ride up in the midst of a full-length dive, whereas nowadays there's nothing further from our minds.

While the English response to this perceived problem ran to a few extra inches added to the bottom of a goalies' jersey, the German approach was more comprehensive.

Studying the ever-changing range of keepers-only kit in our vintage Uhlsport catalogues, we came across evidence of this fleetingly fashionable under-trunk shirt-tail anchoring system.

Well, it certainly offered a complete cure to the arguably unsightly 'gapping' phenomemon and all related paranoia. The only downside to the guaranteed gap-free 'torwartpullover' came in the changing room, when team-mates spotted you doing up the press-studs on your grown-up version of a baby's romper suit.

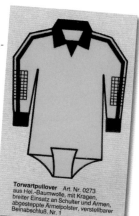

Torwartpullover Art. Nr. 0273
aus Hel.-Baumwolle, mit Kragen,
breiter Einsatz an Schulter und Armen,
abgesteppte Armelpolster, verstellbarer
Beinabschluß. Nr. 1

107

Legends on the line No 7 Stuart Pearce

STUART PEARCE
FOREST

Who knew? 'Psycho' was a frustrated wannabe keeper. From Russia...

Stuart Pearce interviewed in a goalkeeping book? Don't be daft!

When we said we were going to talk to an ex-England international who was one of the heroes at Euro 96, you probably thought we were speaking to David Seaman again. So, why Stuart Pearce? Keep reading to discover all about our superhero left-back's alter ego...

Not a lot of people would know that you played under the guise of a Russian keeper called Yak Jensen while you were contracted to Wealdstone. How did this situation come about, playing for Dynamo Kingsbury Kiev?

"I wanted to play on a Sunday morning with my friends, my schoolmates. To be able to do this in the West Fulham & District League, I had to adopt a false name, as I was already playing for Wealdstone. I played in goal for three and a half years, only stopping because of a broken shin during one of the games."

I read in your autobiography, *Psycho*, that when you were playing in goals you wore bright tangerine and black goalkeeping kit with 'JENSEN' embroidered on the back. And long black shorts down to your knees!

"The real highlight of my time in goal was finishing leading scorer with seven goals! I used to go up for free-kicks, corners and even during free play on occasions. It wasn't like I was really trying to hide my real identity in that get-up – I was bound to get spotted when I threw the ball out to the wing and then chased after it myself, taking on all the opponents!"

I also read that your heroes growing up were Gordon Banks and Peter Shilton – and that you would don the wicket-keeper gloves during the summer, so how did you end up playing left-back?

"Gordon Banks was my first footballing hero, having watched his save against Pele in 1970. I also played wicket-keeper for the electrical engineers at Brent Council. I won my first medal as a youngster as a goalkeeper, so that's how I started. When I started playing a bit more seriously at school it soon became clear I was a better defender than goalkeeper."

Playing in the days with no substitute keepers on the bench, were you always the nominated deputy to don the gloves? If so, did Mr Clough have a view on your goalkeeping ability?

"The first opportunity I had to go in goal was for Wealdstone, playing at Scarborough. I took over the gloves at half-time. At Forest, the only time we lost a goalkeeper during a game, Ian Bowyer went in goal. I guess that tells you Mr Clough's views on my ability as a goalkeeper."

When you were manager at Man City, you opted to stick David James up front against Middlesbrough for the remaining few minutes. How did that all come about, and did you ever consider doing it again with any other goalkeeper?

"I put David James up front in an attempt to unnerve the opposition's defence in the last game of the 2005 season. We needed a win to get a European place. We were drawing with ten minutes to go and we needed to get a goal. James caused havoc, and we did get a penalty. Unfortunately Robbie Fowler missed the penalty!

"I did it with the Under-21s too. I played

> **Sky Blues' latest capture, left back Stuart Pearce was born and lives within the sound of Wembley Stadium, yet when he dreams — as all players do — of treading that hallowed turf, it is as a goalkeeper.**
>
> **Stuart confesses: "I fancy myself a bit as a goalkeeper. I played in goal regularly in Sunday football a couple of years ago and I thoroughly enjoyed it."**
>
> **In fact Stuart's boyhood heroes were England goalkeepers Gordon Banks and Peter Shilton, and when he plays cricket he always pulls on the gloves to play wicketkeeper.**

Joe Lewis for the last 20 minutes against Azerbaijan at MK Dons, as we had run out of outfield subs and got an injury."

"You've played and managed many great goalkeepers, which one stood out the most?

"Peter Shilton and David Seaman would be the two outstanding goalkeepers that I played with. They were the best in the world at the height of each of their careers.

"From a manager's point of view, I signed Joe Hart from Shrewsbury when I was Manchester City manager, who was great value for money considering what he went on to do with both Man City and England."

MY GOALKEEPING HERO

Alan Fettis | Pat Jennings

"I had many goalkeepers that I admired and tried to replicate and learn from. I tried to get something from everyone I watched. Bruce Grobbelaar, because he was different and had charisma. My father was a Linfield fan and took me to watch them when I wasn't playing two games on a Saturday, and the keeper there was George Dunlop. He played about 1,000 games. When I signed for Glentoran I sometimes trained with their first-team keeper Alan Patterson, and loved how he worked. When I started professionally in England, Peter Schmeichel had signed for United and took goalkeeping to another level, so he was the benchmark as a young pro. However, emotionally, with the Irish connection, Pat Jennings would take some beating. And when you meet your heroes you're not always disappointed. Big Pat's a top bloke."

THESE THINGS WERE SENT TO TRY US No.2 Autograph Hunters

It's bad enough when a modern-day shotstopper is minding his own business in Aldi with his missus, or enjoying a romantic meal with his girlriend, and some herbert in a replica top wants a selfie. It's almost enough to make you feel sorry for the lad.

Barry Dawes

You'd think it was a case, like literally everything else, of things being better in the good old days. But back then they had a thing called autograph hunters who collected thousands of scribbled signatures, and would you believe they were actually worse?

Nowadays, you're straight out of the

Laurie Swell

changing rooms and onto the team coach, but back in the day of maximum wage footballers they used to walk out the players' entrance and there'd be 200 jammy-faced kids lying in wait. By the time they finally got the bus home, their tea would be in the dog.

Andy Gray

Here we see Liverpool's poor, wounded Tommy Younger being helped off with what looks like a nasty knock. And yet the vultures are already circling, sizing up the chance to pounce before they shovel him into the waiting ambulance.

THE INTERCHANGEABLE PALMS

In the mid '80s the German brand KKS (Karl Krumbholz Fabrik Für Sportbekleidung) came up with a revolutionary idea that would change the design of goalkeeper gloves forever – or so they thought.

Imagine never having to buy a pair of keeper's mitts ever again. Admit it, the idea has grabbed your attention! Instead, all you'd

need to do is simply buy a pack of new palms to suit any weather condition, stick them on to your gloves with Velcro, and bingo! You can toss away the glovebag, too, while you're at it.

On paper, the design and concept looked great. However, what wasn't factored in was the poor condition of most pitches back in the '80s – thick with mud and sand with just a few blades of grass away in the corners. As

the old joke goes: unfortunately, you don't play football on paper...

I only ever saw one keeper here in England wear them at the time. He was in the RAF, by day a fighter pilot and at weekends our first-choice keeper at Horndean. I was just a young lad in the youth team at this time and, seeing these gloves close up, they looked futuristic and totally exotic. He'd got them over in Germany while stationed there, and always had a big stash of foreign imports in his glovebag to make this young whippersnapper look on in envy.

Fast forward to 2006 when Frank Weigl, now senior product manager at Adidas, was a relative youngster, just starting out at the company. For two years he'd been working on one his first projects to coincide with the release of the F50 Tunit football boot, designed to enable you to change the sole of your boots to suit different weather conditions and a wide variety of playing surfaces. Old-fashioned removable studs just seemed so 20th century.

It's Frank that we have to thank for sharing the story of Adidas's interchangeable palms, which has never previously come to light:

"With the release of the boots, we wanted to do something similar with the goalkeeper," he told us, "with the advantage of this design aiming more for the amateur goalkeeper, who was able to change the

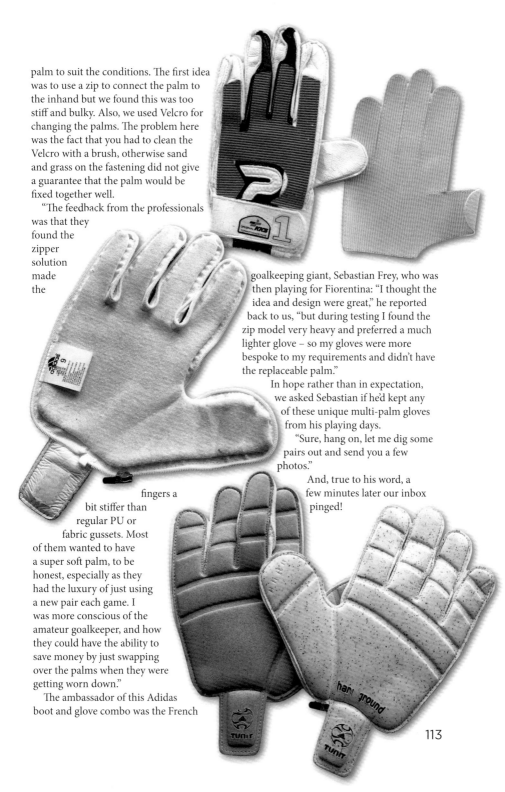

palm to suit the conditions. The first idea was to use a zip to connect the palm to the inhand but we found this was too stiff and bulky. Also, we used Velcro for changing the palms. The problem here was the fact that you had to clean the Velcro with a brush, otherwise sand and grass on the fastening did not give a guarantee that the palm would be fixed together well.

"The feedback from the professionals was that they found the zipper solution made the fingers a bit stiffer than regular PU or fabric gussets. Most of them wanted to have a super soft palm, to be honest, especially as they had the luxury of just using a new pair each game. I was more conscious of the amateur goalkeeper, and how they could have the ability to save money by just swapping over the palms when they were getting worn down."

The ambassador of this Adidas boot and glove combo was the French goalkeeping giant, Sebastian Frey, who was then playing for Fiorentina: "I thought the idea and design were great," he reported back to us, "but during testing I found the zip model very heavy and preferred a much lighter glove – so my gloves were more bespoke to my requirements and didn't have the replaceable palm."

In hope rather than in expectation, we asked Sebastian if he'd kept any of these unique multi-palm gloves from his playing days.

"Sure, hang on, let me dig some pairs out and send you a few photos."

And, true to his word, a few minutes later our inbox pinged!

113

Memorable GOALKEEPING No 7 MOMENTS

DAVE BEASANT
WIMBLEDON 1-0 LIVERPOOL
Date: 14 May 1988
Venue: Wembley Stadium

Fully paid-up Crazy Gang member Dave Beasant became the first keeper ever to save a penalty in an FA Cup final when his homework watching John Aldridge spot-kicks paid off. He didn't dive early as Aldo jinked in, so the Liverpool striker hit it to his left. Gotcha, wack.

Dave was the first goalie to captain his team in an FA Cup final, and by extension the first to lift the trophy in oversize latex gloves.

Less romantically, he was also the first to get paid in goalkeeper gloves for doing both!

But there's no denying 'Crazy' Dave had his softer side, as revealed in his autobiography: "As I stood facing Princess Diana with the FA Cup gleaming between us, it all seemed too good to be true. I kept thinking that I'd wake up at any second to discover that it had all been an incredible dream. I'd fantasised about this moment a hundred times but now it was for real – I was about to receive the coveted trophy from a true-to-life princess..."

Big Dave lifts the cup...

THE HARLEM GLOBETROTTERS v GOALKEEPERS UTD

Back in May 1975 a sporting spectacular took place at Wembley's Empire Pool, the likes of which had never been seen before.

In an inter-sport mash-up that made Mixed Martial Arts' boxing/kung-fu/wrestling crossover look like a completely sensible idea, a team of star goalkeepers were invited to take on the greatest basketball team in the world. At basketball.

For younger readers, the Harlem Globetrotters were a major box-office draw back in the '60s and '70s, and would sell out venues all over the world. Many of their players were household names at the time,

with stars such as 'Meadowlark' Lemon and 'Curly' Neal even appearing in a *Harlem Globetrotters* animated cartoon series which was successfully exported to UK television

screens.

Phil Parkes, then of QPR & England, was on the goalies' tallball team, so we asked him how it had come about.

"Bob Wilson got in touch with us all," Phil revealed, "and said, 'Do you fancy a game of basketball against the Harlem Globetrotters? They're coming over to do some exhibition games.' Like a shot, I said 'yes', as these guys were world famous, and even having a photo with them was more than enough for me."

Bob was working for the BBC at the time, and it turns out he'd been asked if he could get a team together as half-time entertainment for one of the nights.

So how did the big match turn out? Presumably not well, given that none of the Goalies side – Dickie Guy, Jim Cumbes, Mervyn Day, Ray Clemence, Phil and Bob himself – had ever played basketball before in their lives!

"It was a pretty one-sided affair, to be honest, as you would expect," Phil admitted. "In fact, we didn't even get paid to play in the game, it was just an honour to meet these guys."

The final word must go to Bob Wilson, organiser of the historic event:

"All I can remember is that I put the team together," he smiles, "and we got thumped that night!"

GK BRAND PROMO CARDS

In the secretive world of collectors, those in the know hoard and dote over the goalkeeping brands' promotional postcards that used to come with a pair of gloves, or were sent out to autograph hunters. These highly sought-after keeper-only cards neatly trump commonplace Panini and Topps collections. If only they'd produced custom albums to keep them in – now, that would have been really special.

Erik Thorstvedt

BORUSSIA Mönchengladbach
als freundliche Erinnerung

PUMA

TURN IT ON. PUMA

IAN WALKER

reusch

Unfair advantage, ref! Tottenham's Ian Walker sprouts an extra pair of hands.

adidas

Shay Given
NEWCASTLE UNITED & REPUBLIC OF IRELAND

uhlsport

Eva Russo

116

Heinze-Torwartausrüstungen

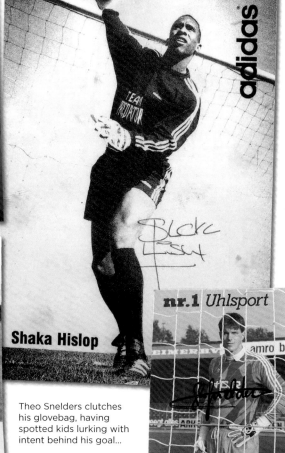

adidas

Shaka Hislop

GARY BAILEY CLOTHING

STAR / Sukan Sports

nr.1 Uhlsport

Theo Snelders clutches his glovebag, having spotted kids lurking with intent behind his goal...

adidas

ANDONI ZUBIZARRETA
Selección Nacional

reusch

117

Troels Rasmussen

hummel

BRUCE GROBBELAAR
(LIVERPOOL F.C.)

DUNLOP
Sports Footwear

HI-TEC

Mark Crossley

Bruce! Great if you can just hold that pose for five more seconds, please?

reusch
Torwarthandschuhe
Michael Serr

KARLSBERG

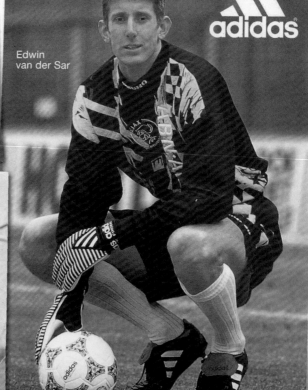

adidas

Edwin van der Sar

Sondico

NEVILLE SOUTHALL

Best wish
Neville Southall

118

PHILATELIC PERKS

How ironic that the small pieces of paper that obsess and delight blokes all over the globe should be known

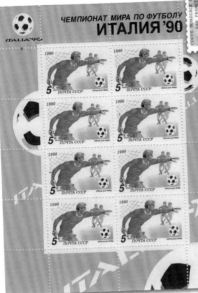

And, sure enough, along with football cards, programmes and a hundred other supposedly disposable snippets of history, stamps have a great nostalgic story to tell. The earliest stamp in our collection features the flying orange keeper overleaf – sure enough, it's an Air Mail special for

as 'ephemera'. The mere suggestion that postage stamps, like promotional

the Italian Colonies dating back to the 1934 World Cup. What's next? The blue 1938 World Cup stamp, again issued by the host nation to commemorate the tournament.

cards, equipment catalogues and goalkeeper-related cereal packets should have been designed for a fleeting, or 'ephemeral', existence triggers an age-old response in many a grown-up little boy: I'll keep that; I'll start a collection.

Beyond the post: Brazil celebrates the 1982 World Cup in Spain.

Liechtenstein are next in line, with a heroic 25-cent sepia shotstopper presumably issued to compensate the locals for not having

had a national team to play in neighbouring Switzerland in 1954.

Produced for the collector market, the single-stamp Hungarian mini-sheet above was issued to mark the 1962 World Cup in Chile. The Magyars did reach the quarters, no surprise with keeping of this quality.

We guess you might have spotted one of the three GB 1966 commemoratives on the previous page. But here's the big question: was that meant to be Gordon Banks, or was it just a coincidental lookalike?

Two more mini-sheets mark Mexico '70, from Yemen and Ajman, again produced to catch the eye of small boys rather than for practical purposes. And that's the way we like it. Much more fun than the functional

stamps from Malta and West Germany for World Cups '74 and '78. What's our pick of the album? It's got to be the *Roy of the Rovers*-style Belgian mini-sheet for France 98. You've got to love a goalkeeping collectable that features a green GK jersey with a pink hoop!

A French commemorative marking the third ever World Cup, hosted on home soil.

GLOVE BRAND: SONDICO

In the '80s and '90s the Football Leagues in England and Scotland were marvellously well stocked with top-name keepers, many of whom appeared on the Sondico Sports roster. Having the three England keepers – Clemence, Shilton and Corrigan – in the glovebag good and early paved the way for more stars to follow over the years.

Flicking through the 1991/92 advertising literature, it lists no less than 70 goalkeepers in the Sondico stable, including names such as Neville Southall, Chris Woods, Nigel Spink, Tony Coton and Nigel Adkins of

When the double 'SS' logo graced the hands of Football League keepers by the bucketload.

Wigan. Oh, come on. You all knew Nigel was a keeper before moving on to be a physio and then a manager, didn't you?

With eleven full internationals on the books, Sondico certainly gave Uhlsport and Reusch a run for their money during these periods. And the outfield offering was none too shoddy, either, with shinpads and balls endorsed by the likes of Gary Lineker, Bryan Robson and Ian Rush,

England's Top 3

choose the number 1 Gloves!

Sondico

Then there was the Nigel Spink Pro in the 1992/93 collection, with its graffiti palm in supersoft latex, its embossed logo and wrist protection retailing at a tasty £42.95.

And who can remember the 'octopus latex-palmed' Tony Coton Classic which provided excellent ball adhesion and extra durability. We'd actually never spotted the octopus reference before. True enough, eight arms would give any keeper quite an advantage; but we can't help wondering how many squid they would have cost?

Saving the best 'til last, we've had to expand the Sondico section in true 'Stop Press' style to make room for this latest historical discovery.

I recently purchased some old sports

to name but three huge draws.

While trawling the Sondico catalogue archives, a few notable gloves stood out.

The Sondico Solar featured a polka-dot suction palm which, when put to the test during a match, sucked up less of the ball than it did mud and sand from the goalmouth.

Sondico Sports Goalkeeper Gloves
AS RECOMMENDED BY PETER SHILTON Notts Forest and England Goalkeeper
MENS

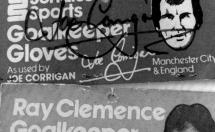

Sondico Sports Goalkeeper Gloves
As used by JOE CORRIGAN — Manchester City & England

Ray Clemence Goalkeeper Gloves
Sondico Sports — Liverpool and England Goalkeeper
YOUTHS

trade magazines off eBay that dated back to 1980, and in one of them was an advert which truly stopped me in my tracks...

A pair of Sondico Sports gloves complete with an 'S' on the back hand. Surely not? I'd heard rumours that this hybrid crossover had once existed but had never seen any evidence to confirm the fact.

A quick call to Dave Holmes and a search of his archived correspondence led me to a letter from Reusch that they'd sent to Dave in July 1980 – this because he, too, was thinking of using the 'S' glove (see page 62/63).

This glove in the photo below, alongside the 32-panel ball, was a sample design that was never officially released. Eventually, Sondico went for a different option,

as a very similar style of glove was already being produced as part of the Reusch range. What needs to be pointed out here is that

Reusch were making the higher-quality gloves for Sondico at this time, over in Germany, while the lower-quality pairs were being produced in Hong Kong and India by a different manufacturer.

On consideration, Reusch felt it wouldn't be right to produce them for Sondico Sports, as this would have impacted directly on their own glove range, already being worn by the likes of Toni Schumacher in Germany.

All we need to know now is what happened to this sample pair, and whose attic they're currently stored away in.

Left: Martin Jarvis guards his near post, as far as the muddy puddle will allow.

Above: Lance Thomson gets perilously close to the three-bar fire in his Admiral England shirt.

KID GLOVES

Once again we put out the call on Twitter and the Got, Not Got blog asking you to go to your parents' houses and raid their photo albums for evidence of your youthful goalkeeping prowess. And again you delivered like a 70 yard goal kick that hits the chest of the target man.

Many thanks to everyone who sent in their photo, we wish we could have used them all.

Above: Scott Fletcher models an Ipswich Town goalie jersey and Reusch gloves.

Far left: Samuel Pavlik explores an adventurous palette.

Left: Alistair Ramsay, sporting Hummel 'Peter Schmeichel' shirt and rabbit's ears. Never gets old.

Far left: Eddie O'Mahoney is the Candy man.

Left: Justin Pannell and his Sondico glovebag.

Centre: Adam Cordery and his dog.

Below: Marc Smith ever vigilant, despite the rain.

Bottom left: Mark Taylor sports a classic local shirt ad.

Bottom centre: Daniel Cox, who is taller than a fence.

Bottom right: Jerry Boekel gets the pose just right.

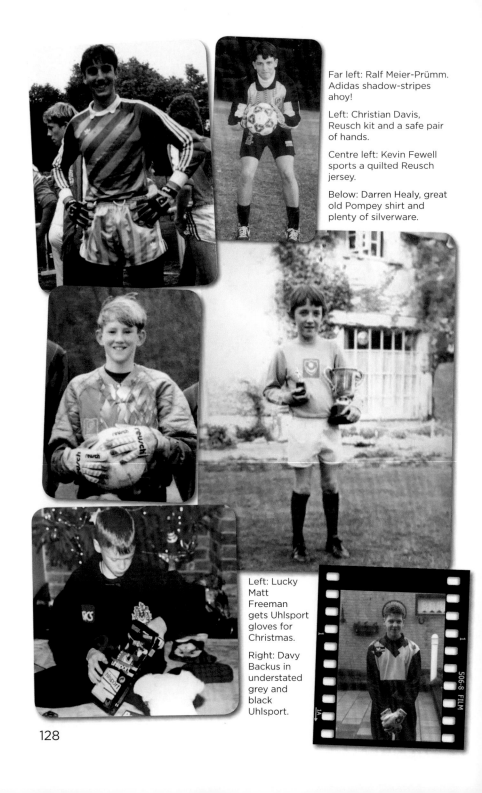

Far left: Ralf Meier-Prümm. Adidas shadow-stripes ahoy!

Left: Christian Davis, Reusch kit and a safe pair of hands.

Centre left: Kevin Fewell sports a quilted Reusch jersey.

Below: Darren Healy, great old Pompey shirt and plenty of silverware.

Left: Lucky Matt Freeman gets Uhlsport gloves for Christmas.

Right: Davy Backus in understated grey and black Uhlsport.

Left: Paddy Short is the Player of the Year.

Above: Chris Holland

Right: Geoff Wyatt in old school Bonetti Gloves and 70s tracky.

Above: Manfred Tschenett combines goalkeeping and rambling.

Left: Marc Smith (again) shows off his Christmas loot.

And finally, in the silver corner right: Ron Rushing in Reusch and far right: Wayne Roberts in the Umbro England strip.

129

CORINTHIAN CUSTODIANS

Last time around, we threw down the gauntlet to obsessive goalkeeping collectors of a certain age with our revelation (-painted plastic). In no time at all, Craig casually pulled from his impressive collection our long-lost figures of Tony Roberts, Tony Coton and Alan Miller.

We asked Craig why these particular models never made it to the shelves of Woolworths and other high-street outlets.

"Basically, models were cancelled due to a variety that various Corinthian figurines of shot-stopping stars were modelled and produced back in the '90s, but then never given an official release.

Well, thanks to Craig Robinson of the fantastic Corinthian Archive website, we can now give you a insider's glimpse of the super-rare big-head tributes, which must all be worth their original models' weight in gold of reasons," he explained. "Players moving clubs, or the sculpture wasn't approved. Poor sales from the initial range, so additional figures were cancelled, or the club got relegated because they were no longer in the Premier League."

The truth can be hard to swallow. Just imagine how it would feel to have a two-inch-tall likeness of your good self wiped out

remember ever wearing a blue Cellnet-sponsored top!"

We also chased down Tony Coton, who was playing for Sunderland in the fateful season of 1996/97, though previously of Birmingham City, Watford and Manchester City fame. Faced with his own mini effigy, Tony was quick to quip: "What a handsome chap I was! Although I think Humpty Dumpty was modelled on me!"

By now, the eye of many a collector will have drifted to the bottom of the spread, where the array of Corinthian GKs will be in danger of causing high blood pressure, or worse.

That's right, not one of these figures ever made it into production in the form you see below. They were all custom painted by the talented Marc Brine, who also made the cool micro glovebags – just for us.

on the basis of such criteria.

We got in contact with Alan Miller to let him know of our findings – he had to be top of our list of priorities, given that the former Middlesbrough keeper had been so upset by his narrow missing out on injection-moulded megastardom.

"That's brilliant!" Alan cheered. "I can now get a decent night's sleep. They definitely got the quiff right at that time. I can sort of see a resemblance, but I dont

PARKES

Hunkered down in Phil Parkes' Berkshire living room, it didn't take long for the conversation to turn to glorious goalkeeping memories.

Phil started out at Walsall in 1968, before moving to QPR in 1970 for £15,000, then on to West Ham for £565,000 – a world record fee for a goalkeeper at that time, in 1979. He finished his career at Ipswich and then coached at Town and QPR.

Phil's single England cap could have been many more, specifically if Don Revie hadn't gone back on his word

against Wales in 1976.

But let's kick off by talking about Cossack! Do you still have any cans in the loft?

"Ha ha, no. I never wore it, to be honest, only in the advert. A friend of mine knew someone in the trade and told me they were looking for a footballer to take over from Roger Clark, the rally driver. The advert took three days to film: a scene in the changing room, complete with smoke machine; a trip to the park in Northolt with my wife, Lavinia, and the kids going up down a slide; and then at the Leicester City game. The ad director didn't know a lot about football. He asked if I could save a penalty for the cameras during the game! Then, amazingly, Leicester did get a penalty. I dived to my left to keep it out from Frank Worthington, and they ended up using the footage in the commercial.

1972-73

1973-74

PORTUGAL

I had a Cossack badge sewn to my jersey, too, for the rest of the season!"

You were one of the first UK keepers known for wearing latex-palmed gloves...

"We played Borussia Mönchengladbach in a pre-season friendly back in 1975, and I was wearing my green cotton gloves. The heavens opened before the game. My opposite number, Wolfgang Kleff, approached me before kick-off and said, "Here, try a pair of these, I think you'll find they're much better than what you're

wearing." I'm thinking, is he having me on here? Are they going to be like a bar of soap? Complete opposite. They were incredible! After the game, Dave Sexton went in their dressing room and purchased six pairs from him."

Before you started up Sukan Sports with Dave Holmes you were the poster boy for Starcraft's Metric gloves and Asics boots...

"That's correct, Starcraft had a range of 'P' gloves to be sold in my name alongside the existing Peter Bonetti range. The Asics boots were fantastic, made to measure from kangaroo leather. But the gloves weren't the greatest, to be honest. Uhlsport were far better. Back then, cameras weren't at every game so it was quite easy to wear the gloves without anyone spotting. However, that season we ended up getting to the FA Cup final at Wembley. Trying not to upset Starcraft, I had to black out the big white 'U' on the 031s with a marker pen, then on top I stuck some Metric branding to cover it up. But during the game that came off, so those with good eyesight can see this during the

celebrations after the final whistle.

"Also, it was the first time a Sukan Sports yellow glovebag had appeared at a Wembley Cup final. So a good bit of free advertising for the company that day, both of which I still have up in the loft!"

After a third cup of coffee we retired to look through Phil's trophy cabinet – how I'd have loved to try on that England cap! – and to the garden for a memorial photograph of Phil and his infamous Cossack jersey.

MY GOALKEEPING HERO

Alex Williams | Pat Jennings

"I remember a game at City, Francis Lee had a free-kick 30 yards out. He screamed a shot in, we all thought it was a goal. Though hit hard, it went straight to Pat, who twisted the top half of his body and used his shoulder to block the shot, which rebounded out about the same distance out."

THE AMERICAN INVASION

For the better part of two decades, American goalkeepers were a regular presence in England's top flight. This influx began as far back as the 1980s, but hit its stride in the 2000s, with the likes

goalkeepers. In retrospect, it's not difficult to see this as a backhanded compliment. The United States, after all, lacked the coaching, national development resources and simple passion for the game required to produce a world-class midfielder or striker. But home-grown American sports all required a level of hand-eye co-ordination which lends itself well to goalkeeping.

That, at least, has always been the orthodox explanation. I have another: goalkeeping is almost an individual sport within a team sport, which holds a special appeal for American athletes. The US goalkeepers who found success in Europe were singularly driven individuals. Each wanted to test himself at a higher level. Each was willing to fly to a country where they knew almost nobody, and where

of Tim Howard, Brad Friedel, Kasey Keller, Marcus Hahnemann, Juergen Sommer and Ian Feuer racking up over 1,000 Premier League appearances between them. But how did a country that struggled to compete at international level produce so many top-flight goalkeepers? And why did they choose to cross the Atlantic to ply their trade?

In the 1970s, Pele himself had predicted that the first American stars would be

any accomplishments in the domestic game meant nothing. Each was willing to walk into a dressing room where their accent was going

to put them in an instant credibility deficit.

I know exactly what that's like, because I did it myself in 1987.

I had spent the previous year with the Orlando Lions, where my manager, Mark Dillon, stressed to me that I needed to get across to England to develop. I didn't really need further prompting. Mark had some connections, and he secured me a trial with non-League Borehamwood FC. It wasn't glamorous, but it was a physically and mentally demanding level in a football-saturated culture. It was, then, exactly what I

needed. Uncapped at senior level, I had no chance of securing a work permit, so despite a successful debut for Borehamwood and an extended trial with Brentford, my England dream never reached a higher level than non-League. But it improved me as a goalkeeper, and led to successful seasons back home in the still-struggling professional leagues prior to MLS.

While the first wave of American keepers in England found success, they're now all gone, which concerns some in the US; but one simple consideration is that Americans no longer need to leave home to have a decent professional career. No such opportunity in MLS existed for me in the '80s, but that would not have mattered. For me and so many other American goalkeepers, England was our spiritual home. It was where we wanted to be, and we were coming over no matter what.

With thanks to Justin Bryant, author of Small Time: A Life in the Football Wilderness.

LET ME SHOW YOU MY HEROIC KEEPER POSE

When I was a junior shotstopper, I didn't just want to grow up to be a dependable professional six-foot shotstopper who played for Portsmouth & England.

Much more than that, my

to help capture images for an imaginary portfolio of suitably dashing, dangerous, diving action shots.

Tipping over. Rising above an imaginary goalmouth melee. Claiming and clasping.

The optimistic past master still lives in eternal hope.

admirably focused ambition was was to be the kind of all-action shotstopper who also got his fanciful mid-air image on the cover of the matchday programme.

To this end, I would practice for long hours launching myself on the lawn, sometimes enlisting the help of my brother, dad and trusty family Kodak

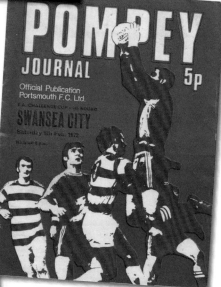

136

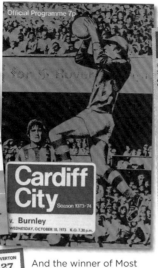

Official Programme 7p

Cardiff
City   Season 1973-74

v. Burnley
WEDNESDAY, OCTOBER 10, 1973 K.O. 7.30 p.m.

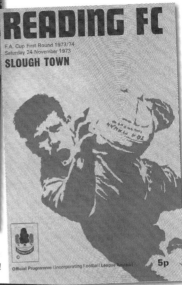

READING FC

F.A. Cup First Round 1973/74
Saturday 24 November 1973
SLOUGH TOWN

Official Programme Incorporating Football League Review   5p

No 12091

LEEDS UNITED A.F.C.   EVERTON 27
TOKEN   1969-70

OFFICIAL PROGRAMME
ONE SHILLING

LEEDS
UNITED
VERSUS
EVERTON
SATURDAY, 27th DEC., 1969   K.O. 3.0 p.m.

NEXT HOME
MATCHES   SATURDAY, 3rd JANUARY, 1970 K.O. 3.0 p.m.
SWANSEA TOWN
F.A. CUP — THIRD ROUND
SATURDAY, 10th JANUARY, 1970 K.O. 3.0 p.m. C.L.
WEST BROMWICH ALBION RESERVES

And the winner of Most
Dynamic Cover Keeper for
1973 goes to... Reading FC!

SCOTLAND v
FINLAND

HAMPDEN
PARK

21 OCT. 1964

WORLD CUP QUALIFYING
INTERNATIONAL (First Match)

OFFICIAL
PROGRAMME

KICK OFF
7·30 p.m.
price 1/-

FULHAM
FOOTBALL CLUB

OFFICIAL
PROGRAMME 6D

SEASON 1966-7 LEAGUE DIVISION ONE
SHEFFIELD UNITED
SATURDAY 3 SEPTEMBER 1966 KICK OFF 3 PM

GLOVE BRAND: KKS & KRÄNZLE

Here are two German brands that remain something of an enigma to us. Our knowledge of both the companies and their products remain full of holes, as all attempts to research the gloves have been met with closed doors – which just makes us all the more curious! Please do get in touch if you can shed any more light, and we'll share the information with a waiting world of borderline compulsive former cats.

KKS – or Karl Krumbholz Fabrik Für Sportbekleidung, when they were on the naughty step – were based in Schwabach,

number one. Sepp Maier famously wore them in the 1974 and 1978 World Cups. Yes, the classic oversized

gloves with 'S' and 'M' on the backhand.

KKS also later produced a range solely for Patrick, which Peter Schmeichel could be seen wearing in his early days in Denmark and in conjunction together with dual branding. And the company take full responsibility for the interchangeable-palm gloves we featured earlier in the book.

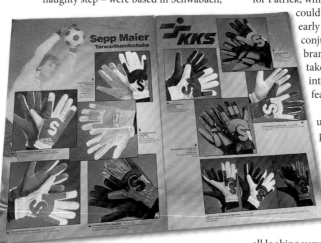

Germany. Founded in 1928, the company operated in the import/export industry, producing textiles and clothing – including goalkeeper gloves for Germany's undisputed

Kränzle were not established until 1949, when they started producing whole kit ranges, from jerseys and shorts to caps and gloves.

Celebrating their 25th anniversary, the 1974 catalogue has endorsees Wolfang Fahrain, Wolfgang Kleff and Gerhard Heinze all looking very dapper, the former seemingly lending inspiration to Cadbury's for their Milk Tray adverts of the time.

Kleff later moved on to endorse Uhlsport and Reusch while Heinze, along with Dieter Scheiffele, set up the Heinze Sportartikel

company in Stuttgart to take over the selling of Heinze products to the sports trade. The first Heinze gloves that we're aware of had the 'H' on the back, like the ones Ubaldo Fillol wore in the 1978 World Cup. His gloves had two uprights going down two fingers, and then a stripe like a crossbar joining the two to make the capital 'H'. Later, this evolved into a single upright with a curved arch to the lower part, forming a lower-case 'h', the logo that was used for the Heinze clothing range.

The gloves may have looked simple and basic compared to the gloves of the present day, but these were the best on the market at the time. Without doubt, the German companies were leading the way in the field of goalkeeping research and development.

GET SHIRTY

It's a rare and treasured privilege to be able to leaf through a vintage keepers' equipment catalogue, an innocent pleasure that I never take for granted.

After a hard day's work and long

Gary Bailey, or an underhit backpass in a disastrously muddy cup match circa 1989.

It's been part of the pleasure of putting together the *Glove Story* books, sharing these images in the knowledge that other keepers will experience a similar flood of virtual emotions brought on by a heavily quilted cotton jersey; by a Reusch shirt modelled by

commute, or with a big mug of coffee on a Sunday morning, what a nostalgic treat it is to search out an old favourite catalogue full of goalkeeper gloves, jerseys and other esoteric equipment, and relax in an insulated fog of rose-tinted memories. So many images subconsciously trigger a specific emotion of a time and place. I had them. I wanted one of those so badly. And here's a shirt that instantly brings to mind

David Seaman, or by forgotten sports shop dreams of a Sepp Maier jersey with an asymmetric stripe.

The original catalogues are becoming ever harder to find,

900001 Emerald
900002 Amber (illustrated)
900003 Scarlet

Admiral

Peter Shilton originals

tracksuits

for boys and youths. As worn by the England goalkeeper himself. 100% stretch nylon. Hard-wearing, easy to wash, non shrink. 12 month 'fair wear' guarantee. Contrast pants with striking stripes. Roll necks. Peter Shilton crest. Small boys, boys, and youths (See tracksuit measurement chart.)

Goalkeepers jerseys

personally designed by England's Number One keeper. 100% cellular nylon. Snug-fit turtle neck. Non-restricting sleeves. Peter Shilton badge on chest. Colour choice now includes Peter's famous all-white version. Small boys, boys, youths: small men's, men's, large.

Complete Gift Pack

contains white PS jersey with matching white shorts and socks plus black knitted gloves. Full size range.

these days. And, of course, not every ex cat has the inclination to spend every spare moment hunting down deliciously damp-smelling pamphlets.

Here's hoping there's a shirty memory here that whisks you back in time – and that the muddy moment it deposits you

900011 Emerald/Black
900012 Amber/Black
900013 Scarlet/Royal
900014 Sky/Black
(illustrated)

in, back in the '70s/'80s/'90s, involves penalty heroics rather than a ball stuck in the mud in your 'D', and a self-righteously incandescent centre-half.

Hmm – just me, that one?

Goalkeeper Jerseys & Shorts

Sizes: BOYS · YOUTHS · SMALL · MENS · LGE MENS · EX LGE

EDDIE NIEDZWIECKI 'AUTOGRAPH'

CHRIS WOODS 'AUTOGRAPH'

IAN ANDREWS 'SHADOW STRIPE'

TRAINING TROUSERS

DAVID SEAMAN 'ESPRIT'

reusch

Sepp Maier Torwartbekleidung

Torwartpullover Art. Nr. 0205

Torwartpullover Art. Nr. 0215

Torwartpullover Art. Nr. 0200

Torwartpullover Art. Nr. 0206

Torwartpullover Art. Nr. 0210

Top, middle: To save a few bob, look who took over GK modelling duties for Patrick's 'Kevin Keegan' jersey range.

141

Memorable GOALKEEPING MOMENTS No 8

DINO ZOFF
ITALY 3-1 WEST GERMANY
Date: 11 July 1982
Venue: Santiago Bernabéu Stadium, Madrid

Dino Zoff was the first goalkeeper to lift the current World Cup, a feat achieved when he was 40 years young. For anyone who fancies a tilt at the record, the precise length of his tooth was 40 years, 4 months and 13 days.

From our unique perspective, Dino was also the first Uhlsport-endorsed goalkeeper to captain the winning side. And who else could possibly have won the award for goalkeeper of the tournament?

There was just one weeny downside for Uhlsport, and that was Dino's decision to hoist the trophy high with his bare hands, unlike most keepers of today who would grab any opportunity to get their gloves into shot. Even so, the event still provided some great publicity for his cool 034s and 040s.

Interestingly, Gianpiero Combi, also of Juventus & Italy, was the first goalkeeping captain to lift the World Cup; but in 1934 it was the old Jules Rimet Trophy his side won.

HOWZAT! TONY GODDEN AND HIS WICKET-KEEPER INNERS

Having seen many photos and clips from games where Tony Godden, the great West Brom keeper of the '70s and '80s, appeared to be wearing white leather gloves, it was great to finally get a chance to ask Tony about the origins of his unique idea. It's never too late to try out a top tip!

So, what were they and what was the reason for wearing them instead of the latex-palmed gloves that were then coming on to the market?

"You're right," Tony con-firmed. "They were leather. They were the white chamois-leather inners from cricket wicket-keeper gloves. When I first signed for West Brom I was training with John Osborne, and he was wearing a pair; however he wouldn't for a game, just training. He tossed me a pair to try, I gave them a good rinse in the sink and the grip was something else, everything stuck like glue. They were fantastic, and I wore them for many years. Even when the likes of Uhlsport and Reusch gloves were available, I still preferred them. The downside came when it rained, though. They got soaked through and became useless as the water just got absorbed into the leather."

We have Peter Wall to thank for a photo of you taking delivery of a pair of Eaton industrial gloves. Did you ever wear them in a match? I take it the gloves never made it

West Bromwich Albion F.C.
West Bromwich, West Mid's
Mark Taylor,
Tuesday 15th July.
The Mere,
Mill Lane,
Barton-U-Needwood,
Staffordshire.

Dear Mark,

I am very sorry I have not sent you any gloves earlier, but I have been very busy and have just recently spent some time in hospital, first to remove a lump on my wrist, then I had bad stomach trouble.

I am sending you the same gloves that I wear in matches. I do hope that this makes up for the delay. I should very much like to come to one of your matches, but, will have to find the time from somewhere, what with the season already just around the corner.

All I can say Mark, is practice, practice, train hard, play hard, and one day perhaps, who knows.

Your friend,

Tony.

into full production with your endorsement!

"No, that was really just a photo opportunity to promote Peter's company at the time. "He knew that I was wearing a white pair of gloves, and he got the company logo on a pair of his industrial gloves and presented them to me after a game

one day. Maybe I missed a trick there!"

Cue hundreds of goalies asking for cricket gloves in sports shops, and maybe even begging for cast-offs outside factory gates!

143

EDDIE NIEDZWIECKI SPORTS

Similar to Sukan Sports in terms of stock and the goalkeepers' obsessions to which it pandered, Eddie Niedzwiecki Sports was never based in a shop but instead

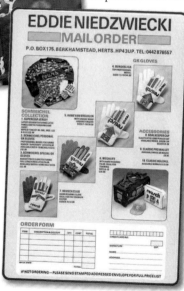

"I was playing for Chelsea at the time and had a contract with Reusch to wear their gloves," Eddie explained the genesis of his business. "I was approached by Bryan Bond, who ran the day-to-day operations for Reusch, along with Andrew Ward, with an idea of doing a mail-order glove service with my name fronting it.

"We advertised in *Match Weekly* with a small selection of gloves and jerseys along with a PO Box number set up locally to my home addresses. The orders would come in, my wife would pop to the Post Office in the morning to collect the post and send the details on to Reusch, who would fulfil the order back to the customer."

Aww, I always thought the packages I received were coming direct from you – sealed, signed and delivered personally

advertised by mail order in football magazines back in the '80s and '90s. The business was run by the Wrexham and Chelsea keeper Eddie, together with his wife, from their home in Hertfordshire.

We caught up with Eddie to talk about those unforgettable, near-hypnotic adverts – and to casually enquire whether he still has a giant stash of priceless vintage gloves and jerseys in his back bedroom...

"Dear Eddie, Can you help? I am seeking keeper gear in shades of purple or luminous yellow..."

by the gloved hand of Eddie Niedzwiecki!
"The process worked really well," Eddie kindly decides to let me down easily, "apart from the odd time where Reusch didn't have a particular glove or jersey in stock, or a package went astray in the post; but apart

from that we gave it a good go and it worked well."

Bring it back, Eddie! Never say never...

145

THESE THINGS WERE SENT TO TRY US No.3 Him Again...

It came as quite a shock to Gordon Banks when he was transfer listed by Leicester City back in 1967. After all, he was widely recognised as the greatest goalkeeper on the planet, and fittingly had just helped England to lift the 1966 World Cup. Meanwhile, Peter Shilton was just a 17-year-old understudy with the crazy idea that he wanted to play for the first team.

As Gordon told us, the move really shook him, affecting his children, friends and the settled social scene he enjoyed with his wife.

But Stoke City presented a bright new challenge for the England keeper... until that career-wrecking car crash in 1972.

Even so, when Shilts followed him to Stoke in '75, Banks was on hand to resume sharing his knowledge and skills. What a man.

EVERY BOY'S DREAM - THE PORTABLE GOAL

Endorsed by stars such as Peter Shilton, Gordon Banks and Peter Bonetti back in the day, the garden goal was strictly the stuff of dreams, at least in the Stokes household. Given the prices – crikey, seven quid even in the days before we went decimal! – it definitely wasn't one of those items that made it on to the Christmas list along with the customary *Roy of the Rovers Annual* and pair of gloves.

While some spoilt junior netminders doubtless found themselves the proud owner of no less than two portable goals, groundsman and star player in their own garden lawn-based stadium, us mere mortals were forced to make do with playing between handily spaced trees, or balancing bamboo canes in precarious approximations of a goal frame, tied together with green garden string.

The canes worked fine until someone hit the post or bar, at which point the whole kit and kaboodle was swept away into the middle pen of the Kop,

World Cup 1982

A more permanent solution arrived out of the blue one weekend when my dad decided to knock up a custom portable goal for me and my brother, which wasn't really portable in any way as it weighed a ton and was firmly nailed down on the lawn.

My dad was a carpenter by trade, so it was fairly easy for him to fashion a sturdy goal to

keep us entertained, complete with splinters and chicken wire.

Other than trying to keep the ball out of the chicken wire (sorry, the onion bag), it was also required for me to stop the ball missing the goal and hitting the flower beds. Many a game ended when my dad saw us trampling over his prize roses in desperation to retrieve the plastic Wembley Trophy ball from the clutches of the prickly thorns – themselves the cause of nearly as many abandonments as the ball sailing over the hedge into Mrs Bowles' garden, next door.

Looking at these wonderful old-school

aka the laurel bush by the back window. But no worries. It only took ten minutes to rebuild and tie together another bamboo-cane lobster pot.

adverts in more detail today, I still can't believe we didn't spot the "10 days money back offer" that was dangled enticingly before every ten-year-old goalie-in-waiting,

that struggled to contain one of my brother's blockbusters, sent the whole kit back, and even reclaimed the postal order.

The clever things you think of after the event, eh?

like a carrot suspended in front of a donkey's straw hat.

To think, we could have enjoyed a week and a half's worth of "shooting and saving fun with envious pals," and then claimed to have been only partially impressed with a net

TONKA PROSTARS

Big kids of a certain age may remember the Tonka adverts that reappeared before Christmas every year back in the '70s. Over a rumbling tribal drumbeat, a deep voice intoned: "Tonka Toys... Real tough toys, for real tough boys."

No, they didn't mean these little posable football figurines. Tonka were chiefly known for their big, industrial-strength construction vehicle toys.

With all due respect to Spinky, Packie, Grob and and co, their emergence in 1989 as part of an all-kicking, all-diving Sportstar set was probably something of an afterthought. But the rare ones can still fetch up to £50 each to collectors on eBay today!

Is it just us, or do four of these all-different Tonka Sportstars look suspiciously like Dmitri Kharine?

ZOFF

The Dino Zoff range: exclusively for Uhlsport.

The coolest goalkeeper ever to pull on black or grey; the veteran of 570 Serie A matches and 112 for Italy; and now Dino Zoff speaks exclusively for *Glove Story 2...*

In the 1982 World Cup final, why did you switch at half-time from Uhlsport 034 gloves to 040s?

"Actually, I don't remember. Maybe I could have changed them, but there weren't so many differences. The 1982 gloves were very similar to 1978's ones. The biggest changes arrived in the late '70s, when the ball became black and white. Before then the gloves were covered in rubber, such as that used for ping-pong paddles. In those years, in fact, we wore gloves only when it rained."

Did Uhlsport ever question why you didn't keep your gloves on when you lifted the Cup?

"No, there have not been problems. Nobody worried about this kind of thing at the time. Everything was more spontaneous, whereas now it's already planned. Marketing is part of the show. Anyway, I couldn't have worn the gloves when I lifted the trophy because I lost them during celebrations. There were so many people on the pitch and I lost them."

What was your first pair of gloves and how did you come by them?

"I started to use gloves when I was playing for Marianese, the team of my little town: San Mariano del Friuli. They procured them for me."

Was it hard, switching from bare hands to wearing gloves?

"Actually I never had a problem in playing with bare hands when the ball was dry. Instead, it wasn't easy when it was very cold and especially when it rained. In those situations we used to wear gloves of cloth, that weren't ideal. So of course I saw the benefits with the new kind of gloves."

What were your favourite gloves? There's a great story about how you saw Cesena's Lamberto Boranga in the new Italian AM Sport gloves before the 1974 World Cup, and launched a successful newspaper appeal to find out where he got them!

"I've worn Uhlsport for most of my career.

Their gloves were state of the art at the time. They are the ones that I've appreciated most."

When you were Lazio manager, did you ever contemplate signing any British keepers?

"I know that he was from another age, but I really loved Gordon Banks. We met each other in a hotel in Mexico in 1970, just few days before the beginning of the World Cup. He was a great goalkeeper and I was sad the day he died."

How did you become a keeper, and who were your childhood heroes?

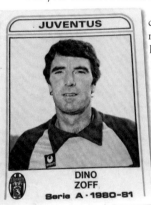

JUVENTUS

DINO ZOFF
Serie A · 1980-81

"When I was a child there was no TV, so I could look to other goalkeepers only in magazines like *Il Calcio Illustrato*. Maybe Lucidio Sentimenti – better known as 'Sentimenti IV' – was one of the most beloved. Then, on the day of my retirement, I had the luck to meet Lev Yashin, who came to see me. He's still the only goalkeeper that won Ballon d'Or, so it was really an honour.

"Anyway, I've always been a goalkeeper, since I was four or five years old. I used to play with my friends on the street. I was good, so also the older children called me to play with them!"

MY GOALKEEPING HERO

Dan Bentley | Gianluigi Buffon & Iker Casillas
"There are a few names that stick out for me. Peter Schmeichel redefined goalkeeping in his own way and I really admire that, but I think the two greatest goalkeepers ever are Iker Casillas and Gianluigi Buffon. They've pretty much won all there is to win in terms of team and individual accolades, and they've both been at the pinnacle of football for basically their entire careers."

TO CAP IT ALL

Once a vital mainstay of any keeper's matchday wardrobe, the humble peaked cap has suffered an alarming demotion in recent decades, until nowadays it's most often left gathering dust in the changing-room locker.

There was a time when no goalie would have trotted out on to the pitch without a cap, any more

than he would have faced up to the oppo without a quilted shirt, gardening gloves,

GORDON BANKS
(Stoke City and England)
By common consent, the greatest goalkeeper in the world, a rating he has accepted, since playing such a vital part in England's 1966 World Cup success, with the same modesty as each of the 70-odd caps he has since 1963. Born in Sheffield, he made his League debut for Chesterfield in 1958-59 and was soon snapped Leicester with whom he got two F.A. Cup final losers' medals before costing Stoke £50,000 in March is a pre-match warm-up routine which has been likened to a one-man Haarlem Globetrotters show. led an O.B.E. while on World Cup duty in Mexico. Voted "Footballer of th

water bottle and 17 packs of Wrigley's spearmint gum – not only for chewing, you understand, but also for adding that certain tacky quality to one's spittle, perfect for

expectorating out on to gloves or bare hands, and thus improving one's grip.

Scientifically informed modern keepers explain the rejection by saying a peak can act as a peripheral distraction, even alter your spacial awareness when you're flying through mid air.

So where do they keep their gum nowadays?

154

A-Ha? Pah. Wham!? No, ma'am. It's Portsmouth's Alan Knight and the look that defined 1985.

155

NEVILLE SOUTHALL
EVERTON 2-3 LEEDS UNITED
Date: 25 August 1990
Venue: Goodison Park

"On the opening day of the 1990/91 season we played newly promoted Leeds United at Goodison. It was shit. We were shit. By half-time we were 2-0 down and conceded a third not long after."

You're listening to the voice of Neville Southall, direct from his terrific autobiography, *The Binman Chronicles*.

"At half-time I needed to get out of the dressing room and get my head together, so I left and went and sat down in the goalmouth. People went on about it and said it was a protest, but it wasn't at all. At worst it was badly timed, coming around the same time as my transfer request. I certainly wasn't protesting against Colin [Harvey], who didn't even know about it until that evening."

In typical Nev style, there's a perfectly timed, quirky punchline to the episode:

"I'd actually done the same before at Wimbledon a year earlier and nobody had said a word about it then!"

KARTOON KEEPERS

In the *Glove Story* pages devoted to fictional comic keepers, we focused on the story of Gordon Stewart, aka 'The Safest Hands in Soccer', and his son Rick, aka 'Goalkeeper', both from *Roy of the Rovers.* Then there was also Charlie Carter and 'Tubby' Morton from Roy's own Melchester side, both giants in the field of graphic-art goalies.

But who remembers the cracking story 'This Goalie's Got Guts'? It was a strip that appeared in *Scoop* comic from the off in 1978. Ben Leiper was a part-time footballer for fourth division Mancastor City, as well as a young doctor at a local hospital. Barely a week would go by without him turning up late for a game due to some unfortunate *Casualty*-style incident, only to redeem himself with incredible heroics

'twixt the sticks.

Quite interestingly, like Gordon Stewart Jr., Leiper the Keeper was a character with a curious past. Way back in 1952, *Adventure* comic carried a weekly story of a goalkeeper called Lanky Hutton – also a student doctor – in a strip that was then known as 'It Takes Guts To Be A Goalie!' As a final footnote for obsessives, Ben Leiper is currently an indie-rock band based in Oslo, Norway.

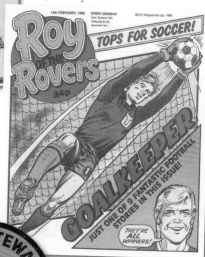

And if you thought those chains of consequences were hard to handle, how about the story of 'Sintek', from *Tiger* comic in the early '80s? Recreated with artificial electronic parts after an accident, the world's first bionic keeper was then signed by ruthless sports promoter Hal Ford, and subbed into a must-win match against Trevor Francis's Sampdoria...

To Be Continued Next Week!

It's tough to perform with kids kicking up the back of your net. Even tougher when you're unsighted for a free-kick from close in.

The big boys take stick from 25,000 on The Kop. But somehow it's worse from four blokes standing behind a rockery.

Pro keepers whinge about crowd and phone flash distractions. How would David de Gea deal with the arrival of the 3.15 to Holyhead?

In the Non-League Laws of Football, this is what they mean by "the angle of the post and bar." In this case, about 83 degrees.

AMERICA'S
PREMIER GOALKEEPER
INSTRUCTOR
GOALKEEPER COACH
☆ U.S. WORLD CUP TEAM ☆

- Video Tape Replay Analysis
- Jugs Shooting Machines
- Fundamental & Advanced Sessions

OTHER GOALKEEPING SCHOOLS

It wasn't just Bob Wilson running residential national goalkeeping schools. One of the pioneers in residential schools was PGL, which began in 1980 with Paul Cooper, Ray Clemence and Bruce Grobbelaar running week-long courses. Simon Dowling went on a residential course in Suffolk in 1981: "A

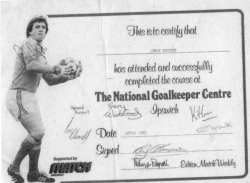

This is to certify that

has attended and successfully completed the course at

The National Goalkeeper Centre

Ipswich

Date

Signed

Editor Match Weekly

Supported by MATCH

former Fulham and Cambridge keeper Malcolm Webster, HQ'd at Oundle School – while down in Portsmouth Peter Mellor's classes held sway. "I went on the Peter Mellor school which was held over

uhlsport NATIONAL
GOALKEEPER SCHOOLS
We're back!

local sports shop even came down to sell us gloves, and I got a pair of Uhlsport 034s and a Ray Clemence Sondico cap. Ray was also a guest visitor who answered our questions and watched us being put through our paces. We even went on a coach to watch the Spurs team do some training at White Hart Lane."

Sondico ran courses with Mervyn Day at the helm, ably assisted by up-and-coming coaches David Coles, Simon Smith and Martin Thomas – plus each course would pull in a Sondico endorsee to chat with the kids and sign autographs.

Uhlsport National Schools were run by

uhlsport

Easter & Summer
1996

Residential Courses
Full Board Arrangements ✓
Home from Home Environment ✓
All Abilities ✓
Constant Supervision ✓
Weekly Keeper Sessions ✓
Qualified Coaching Staff ✓
Celebrity Involvement ✓
One and Two Day Non Residentials ✓

CENTAUR SPORTS

S⃝CCER SCHOOL

**DIRECTED BY
PHIL PARKES – WEST HAM U**

- THE ONLY SOCCER SCHOOL DIRECTED BY A CUR▮ 1st DIVISION PLAYER
- VISITS TO WEMBLEY AND WEST HAM DURING THE
- COLOUR VIDEO PLAYBACK OF COACHING TECHNIQU▮
- FULL EVENINGS ACTIVITIES AND ENTERTAINMENT
- ALL COACHES ARE F.A. APPROVED

TWO 1 WEEK RESIDENTIAL COURSES
31st JULY – 5th AUGUST
7th AUGUST – 12th AUGUST   AT £99.99 INC. VAT.

TWO 1 WEEK NON-RESIDENTIAL COURSE
25th JULY – 29th JULY
1st AUGUST – 5th AUGUST   AT £39.99 INC. VAT.

SEND TO:- CENTAUR SPORTS, 8 PARK ROAD.
CHESHAM, BUCKS. *FOR BOOKING FORM.*

PhilPark Printed in England by The Post Centre, Chesham (0494) 786770

Over in Holland, Frans Hoek was way ahead of his time. Sponsored by Uhlsport and producing coaching videos with the likes of Stanley Menzo and Edwin Van der Sar centre stage, his game-related methods took youth coaching seriously, with great results. "The first camps started in 1984 in my home-town of Hoorn," Frans told us. "The first three courses sold out in two weeks – with around 500 goalkeepers attending!"

Ray ensures that the front-row kids are proudly showing off their Sondico glovebags.

eight evenings at Alexandra Park, on the all-weather pitch," Neil Smithard remembers fondly. "It was brilliant. Peter was there every night which, for an 11-year-old starry-eyed wannabe keeper, was fantastic. We even got a certificate at the end."

In the USA, Dr Joe Machnik started his camps as early as 1977, while Tony DiCicco ran his own SoccerPlus Goalkeeper School. "SoccerPlus was honestly life changing for me as a goalkeeper, as a coach and an overall human," Christian Davis recalls. "You worked your tail off, no doubt, but when Tony showed up it went up to another level."

161

GLOVE BRAND: UMBRO

Umbro have been making fantastic football kits since 1924, when the Humphrey brothers, Harold and Wallace, set up a workshop in Wilmslow, Cheshire.

HumBro – geddit? It's amazing how many of their long-time customers don't!

Goalkeeper jerseys were part of the production line right from the off, manufactured in only the basic colours, though available in specialist lightweight, heavyweight and quilted versions.

In the 1960s, the company kicked off the

trend for producing replica shirts for clubs, having little idea how huge the market would become beyond the era when every adult attended the match on Saturday afternoon

TECHNICAL PRODUCTS 1992

really began to creak open in the British game, and children of all ages were at last given the opportunity to actually become Ray Clemence up the local park, right down to the landmark Hitachi sponsorship emblazoned across their chest.

One of the company's most impressive goalkeeper jersey ranges was the 'Umbro/No1' that was introduced in the 1986/87 season. It included the Mexico, International and Grobbelaar designs – and a logo that was noticeably similar to the Uhlsport Pro badge.

wearing a suit or smart-casualwear with a sensible mackintosh and hat.

Eventually, the commercial floodgates

162

I'm sure there must have been some inspiration drawn from this type of design.

Umbro had moved fairly late into the market for goalkeeper gloves, which they joined in the early 1980s with models for Alan Rough and Bruce Grobbelaar, later expanding the range to include Alex Williams of Manchester City.

The 'Super' model came with an elasticated cuff in PU with the look and feel of kid leather. At least, that what was claimed in the Umbro catalogue. Again, in their words rather than mine, your Supers featured "smooth anti-slip foam finger/palm pad for dry and wet weather grip complete with a ribbed foam back panel, retailing at £14.95."

163

Rough opted for the blue/black colourway, doubtless a reference to Scottish national side, while Grobbelaar went for the suitably Liverpudlian scarlet/black, which came with inside stitching.

The 'Exclusive' gloves had extra quality,

Rough's smooth and superior option came in navy/white, while Grobbelaar's red letter day was heralded in scarlet/white.

Alan Rough wore his 'Super' model at the 1982 World Cup Finals for Scotland, where David Narey's opening rocket famously only succeeded in "making Brazil angry" – four

dimpled palms and adjustable Velcro fastening, but this kind of luxury didn't come cheap. They would set back the flash cat set an extra £2.55

Again following the subtle existing codes,

times. Then we saw Packie Bonner at Italia 90 giving the wild fluorescent style some great exposure when diving to his right to keep out Daniel Timofte's penalty in the dramatic shootout which earned the Republic of Ireland side a place in the quarter-final.

David Seaman continued the World Cup tradition at France 98 and in 2002 in Japan/South Korea; then David James took over the reins for the 2006 and 2010 tournaments.

Looking back, we're irresistibly drawn to the David Seaman gloves marketed with the big bonus of 'Grip Mechanics', an unspecific ingredient that sounded dead good.

"Today's goalkeeper needs to feel confident, whatever the conditions," promised the

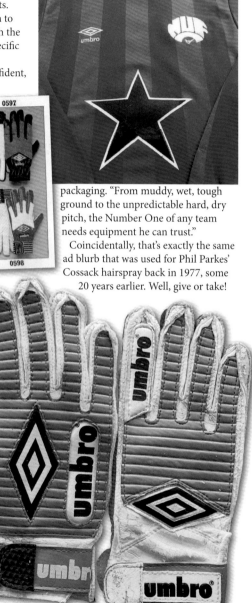

packaging. "From muddy, wet, tough ground to the unpredictable hard, dry pitch, the Number One of any team needs equipment he can trust."

Coincidentally, that's exactly the same ad blurb that was used for Phil Parkes' Cossack hairspray back in 1977, some 20 years earlier. Well, give or take!

WINNER TAKES ALL

In *Glove Story*, we looked back at a formative and character-building episode in my own development, for which I have to thank the uniquely '70s/'80s institution of the write-in prize competition.

A week would rarely go by when you couldn't win the shirt clean off the back of one of your heroes. Occasionally, it was even possible to meet them for a touchingly innocent day out. At least, that was the case

when you were an obsessive serial entrant reading *Shoot!*, *Match Weekly* or *Tiger & Scorcher*. Goodness knows how things worked out when avid young readers of *Wrestling Fortnightly* tried their luck in a free-to-enter funfest.

Mostly, the football comps offered kids the opportunity to act on their private worship of

their soccer heroes, and in turn the pros were happy enough to offload the surplus sundries supplied by their sponsors.

That's easy for me to say. But, as previous readers may recall, I went through mental torture after entering to win Ray Clemence's Admiral England jersey off *Saturday Superstore* – only to see the name of my mate Neil Smithard pulled from the post sack by Spit the Dog.

So near, yet so very far. It was one of the most chastening episodes of my young life. So, what did I do? Swear off the comps and decide to live without the outside chance of meeting Perry Suckling in the flesh?

No, I threw myself into a renewed frenzy of competition entry, all in a crazed attempt to get even, to get recognised, to get a free pair of yellow cotton gloves with a big 'B' on the backhand.

In doing so, I developed a lasting talent for memorising goalkeeping trivia, now a lost art since the advent of Google. Back in the day, there

SHOOT WINNER

CONGRATULATIONS to Matthew Partridge of Tadley in Hampshire who was First Prize winner in our Peter Shilton Argus Press Software competition.

Matthew was invited to London recently to receive his prize of an England signed football and copy of Peter Shilton's Grand Slam computer game, from Mr. Stephen Hall, managing director of Argus Press Software.

was only one way to secure one of 50 pairs of runners-up keeper mitts, and that was often to know against which side Dai Davies had made his Welsh international debut. You couldn't just look it up. And it's just this kind of useless keeper-related info that has served me well in recent years.*

As a goalie comp kid, my reflexes were handily sharpened by hours of waiting for the sound of the postie at the front gate, and then my

20-20 vision was put to the test scouring those lists of winners' names that were always printed in two-point text.

Okay, so I never did get to be the kid in the winner's column pictured with an enviable free cap, or on a day trip to the Potteries in the company of Peter Fox.

But maybe it's true, what your old school team coach used to tell you. It's not the winning, it's the taking part that counts.

Hungary, since you ask. Dai, I'm free any day next week...

SCHUMACHER

Having read *Blowing the Whistle*, the acclaimed 1987 autobiography of Harald Anton 'Toni' Schumacher, I suspect I feel a lot more empathy with him than the majority of the UK and global football fraternity.

The book was translated from the original German version, known as *Anpiff*, which was described as a phenomenal bestseller in West Germany, where it received unprecedented press coverage for a book about a mere shotstopper.

Looking now at the inside cover, you can see why Toni is considered a bit of a splitter among fans:

"Throughout his spectacular career he has never been far from controversy. While his aggressive command of his penalty area and cavalier disregard for his own safety made him the idol of German fans, his arrogance and obsessive will to win have often attracted fierce criticism on the International scene. No more so than during the 1982 World Cup when his heart-stopping challenge on Patrick Battiston left the French player seriously injured, made Schumacher the object of global outrage and fixed him in the minds of football fans throughout the world as the personification of German ruthlessness..."

Ouch! We don't really want to talk about Terrible Toni's bad rep or his book, but rather about his love for all things 'handschue'. Toni made us young cats here in the UK look over the channel with so much envy, especially when he appeared in *Shoot!*, always wearing incredibly exotic gloves. Or, if you were able to stay up late and keep your eyes open to watch *Sportsnight* on a school night, he would often leave you goggling at the screen: *what gloves is he wearing now?!?*

ESPAÑA 82

HARALD
SCHUMACHER
DEUTSCHLAND-BRD

168

Toni's first sponsorship deal was with Heinze, whose gloves and jersey he could be seen wearing for FC Köln against QPR in the '76 UEFA Cup.

He then moved on to Uhlsport for a short period, featuring on the cover of their catalogue for 1978/79 along with the other endorsees.

During that season Toni moved to Reusch, where he stayed loyal for the remainder of his playing career, notably wearing the popular 'S' design against Nottingham Forest in the European Cup semi-final ties.

During his time with Reusch, Toni had a huge influence on the design of his gloves, and over the years there were many wonderful designs and styles, some cracking the English market due to their popularity.

With his original contract in place with his great friend Gebhard Reusch, Toni signed with Adidas just after the 1980 European Championships; however the contract stipulated that the Reusch wording stayed on the gloves, which would continue to be made by Reusch! This resulted in the first dual-branded gloves known to the goalkeeping world – a hot topic raised countless times on keepers' forums.

In the 1982 World Cup the logo was discreetly added to the wrist strap, just below Toni's name. For Mexico '86 he had five different styles prepared; but for all the games he stuck with his favourites featuring the black, red and yellow of the German flag.

It wasn't just gloves that Toni would be remembered for. He also had an array of caps and glovebags, all personalised and very voguish. If there were an award for most stylish keeper of the '80s, there would only have been one possible winner.

Having said that we don't want to focus on Toni's controversial autobiography, it does include one unforgettable admission: "My coach and mother used to worry about my health as I used to do everything at full throttle. Until the day my mother put her foot down. "'That's enough,' she said. 'It's time you moved to a position that doesn't involve so much excitement and running about. Go and play goalkeeper. That'll suit you much better.'

"That's how I became a goalkeeper, on my mother's orders. Because it was a less exciting position to play in. I was eleven at the time."

They do say mum knows best... and in Toni's case, Frau S certainly wasn't wrong.

MY GOALKEEPING HERO

Sebastian Frey | Dino Zoff & Peter Schmeichel

"Dino Zoff for his style - grey jersey, black shorts, black socks - and Peter Schmeichel for his power and determination."

Memorable GOALKEEPING No 10 MOMENTS

**DAVID HARVEY & RAY CLEMENCE
LEEDS UNITED 1-1 LIVERPOOL
(5-6 Penalties)
Date: 10 August 1974
Venue: Wembley Stadium**

Before the game, all the headlines about the first Charity Shield match to be shown live on TV centred on Brian Clough replacing Don Revie and his first game in charge at Leeds.

The headlines after the match were all about the controversial dual dismissal of Kevin Keegan and Billy Bremner, the first Brits to be sent off at Wembley. They'd indulged in a spot of handbags and exited the pitch pathetically, both minus their shirts.

But, from a goalkeeper's perspective, it was all about the penalty shootout. With the scores balanced precariously at 5-5, Leeds bizarrely chose their keeper David Harvey to go next. He duly obliged by thumping the ball over Ray Clemence's bar.

How memorable it was, that friendly GK's Union embrace between David and Ray. David probably thinking, "You're next, Clem, I'll easily save yours" – only for Ian Callaghan to waltz up and win the curtain raiser.

What a lovely picture...

PICKFORD'S GOT BOTTLE

Preparation and analysis are the modern goalkeeping coach's key to success. When it comes to penalties in a major tournament, guesswork is no longer good enough.

At Russia 2018, Jordan Pickford proved the shootout match-winner for England against Colombia; but we asked England GK coach Martyn Margetson what went on behind the scenes.

"The preparation for Russia started 18 months prior," Martyn told us. "The video analysis department painstakingly went through many hours of footage, looking at various penalty situations. We also focused on sports like hockey and rugby to see what information we could learn.

"Once the squads were finalised for Russia we set

JORDAN PICKFORD

about analysing the teams we could be up against, and then looking at different styles, run-up techniques and getting the full analysis

prepared on every player documented. For the Colombia game we knew that when it came down to a pressure penalty situation we were confident that Baca would strike it with his laces, so it was important that Jordan stuck to the information we gave him – and that was to "set and react and don't commit yourself."

How did you get this message across to him?

"We'd prepared by writing down the names of the 18 players that were on the pitch on his water bottle, and for the shootout we scribbled out those that weren't left on the pitch. Each taker had his shirt number and penalty type against it. And just in case Ospina spotted this on his bottle and decided to remove it, we also had backup information written on Jordan's towel – a trick we learned from the England women's hockey team.

"When Eric Dier struck the winning penalty, I celebrated and then made a beeline for the water bottle, to keep as a memento!"

COVERED WITH GLORY

The Peter Shilton programme artwork on the Bristol Rovers cover is our top trump here. It was drawn by none other than Ian Holloway, shortly before he left the Gas for Wimbledon for £35,000 in the summer of 1985.

We asked Ian about his artistic flair. "I've loved my art from a very young age," he said. "I would sit and draw for hours. Diana Ross was a particular favourite! A few of my drawings ended up being on the covers of the Rovers programmes. Gary Mabbutt and Tony Pulis were others I did to go alongside the Peter Shilton one. I drew Shilton as he was the best goalkeeper in England at this time. I guess me doing these drawings saved the club some money, as I never got paid any extra for doing them!"

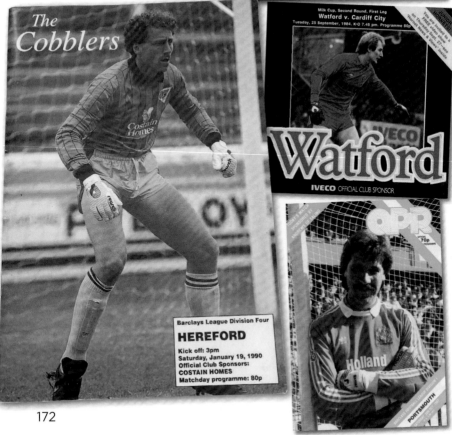

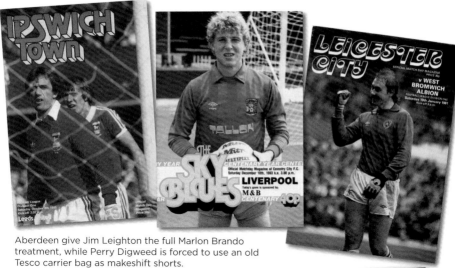

Aberdeen give Jim Leighton the full Marlon Brando treatment, while Perry Digweed is forced to use an old Tesco carrier bag as makeshift shorts.

AUTHORS

Rob Stokes played in goal for Southern League Waterlooville from 1989-98, making 334 appearances and scoring two goals (both penalties!). Rob is a passionate collector of goalkeeping memorabilia, with vintage gloves stretching back to the early '70s. He has a loyal following on Instagram and Twitter – visit @jossiesdad. Derek Hammond and Gary Silke are the authors of 'Got, Not Got', runner-up in the BSBA Football Book of the Year 2012, and the following series. Go to @gotnotgot.

PICTURE CREDITS

Pages 6/7 - Bob Wilson personal collection; 10-12 - Carl Wilkes; 13 - Sukan Sports archive (Alan Rough photo); 14 - Paul Trevillion, original artwork; 15 - Mark Allen (Bruce Grobbelaar and Peter Shilton birthday cards); 16/17 - Robert Wilson original photographs; 18 - Pat Jennings (PJ boot), Rob Richards (PJ logo); 22/23 - Offside picture agency (David James photo); 25 - Brad Pike (Banks jigsaw), Martin Thomas (Frank Swift), Derek Lewens (Peter Shilton); 30 - Mark Allen (Sepp Maier gloves); 33 - Andy Ellis (Mark Wallington); 39 - Sukan Sports archive (2 x Uhlsport gloves); 41 - NorthStandCritic (Subbuteo goalkeeper in nets); 44 - Martin Thomas (Neville Southall Grogg), Sukan Sports archive (Neville Southall artwork); 45 - Robert Wilson (3 x Neville Southall photos); 46 - Simon Mooney Mooneyphoto.com (Peter Schmeichel), Andy Ellis (Joe Corrigan); 52 - Bob Wilson personal collection (David Seaman); 68 - Thanks to David James and to Simon Mooney (mooneyphoto.com) for the photos; 73 - Ian Nannestad (Ron Springett advertisement materials); 73 - Martin Thomas (Ron Springett gloves), Derek Lewens (Ron Springett shop advert); 75 - Mark Taylor (Sondico Sports catalogue page advert); 78 - Thanks to Gary James (Alex Williams); 80/81 - Bob Wilson personal collection; 91 - Alan Knight personal collection; 97 - Alvin Martin (football); 98 - Barry Bell (Sells keyring); 100/101 - Simon Mooney Mooneyphoto.com; 104-106 - Sukan Sports archive; 105 - Thanks to David James for sharing with us his letter to Sukan Sports; 110 - Andy Ellis (Tommy Younger); 112 - Sebastian Frey (gloves and photo); 113 - Darren Morris (Adidas interchangeable palms); 115 - Bob Wilson personal collection (Harlem Globetrotters); 130 - Craig Robinson corinthianarchive.co.uk (3 x master models); 132 Sukan Sports archive (Phil Parkes); 132 - Phil Parkes (caps); 134/135 Special thanks to Tony Davis (Ian Feuer and Kasey Keller photos); 143 - Mark Taylor (Tony Godden shirt and letter), Peter Wall (personal photo with Tony); 145 - Sukan Sports archive (Eddie Niedzwiecki photos); 146/147 - Andy Ellis (Shilton/Banks); 155 - Christian Davis (Reusch Tony Meola cap), Chris Bignell (Peter Bonetti advertising cap card); Simon Dowling (certificate and group photo with Ray Clemence); 158/159 Andy Ormerod; 160 - Roger Watling (Peter Mellor and kids); 161 - Frans Hoek (Uhlsport glove); 165 - Martin Thomas (Newcastle jersey); 168 - Kai Wenzel (Schumacher gloves); 171 - Martyn Margetson (water bottle); 174 - Ralf Meier-Pruemm (Oliver Kahn figure); 175 - Simon Hill (kid diving), Sukan Sports Archive (woman at sewing machine).

174

ACKNOWLEDGMENTS

Special thanks to illustrator Doug Nash. You can find more of Doug's fantastic goalie graphics at TheArtOfGoalkeeping.com and @goalies119, available as posters, T-shirts and original artwork.
Dave Holmes and Martin Thomas for all their help, support and advice.
Bob & Megs Wilson for their hospitality, generosity and invaluable help with contacts and content.
Pete Blackman for his photography work with all the old gloves/bags etc. on location in Portsmouth.
Simon Mooney of mooneyphoto.com.
Marc Brine for his peerless Corinthian figures.
Trevor Brock at Havant & Waterlooville FC, for his hospitality and photographic access to the club.
Dave Bowers for his tales of Bruce Forsyth & co.
Robert Wilson for his kind permission to use unseen photographs from the brilliant 'ONE'.
Carl Wilkes for his priceless collector cards. Visit FootballSoccerCards.com and @rarecards_FCC.
Andy Ormerod for the photos from his Hopping Around Hampshire blog @AndrewRocklob.
Neville Evans & Simon Shakeshaft at the National Football Collection @The_NFC for Flik-Shot.

Authorial contributors: Neil Andrews @goalkeepersdiff, Justin Bryant @Keepers_Union, Denis Hurley @MuseumOfJerseys, Greg Lansdowne @Panini_book, Chris Oakley & Rich Johnson @kitbliss and @footballattic for the Ray Clemence World Cup Game.
Thanks to a whole host of goalkeepers, ex-players, managers and other lovely people who have provided interviews, quotes, photos or contacts: Ian Holloway, Neville Southall, Eddie Niedzwiecki, David James, Jim Rosenthal, Dave Wood & Tony Mills, Alex Williams, John Burridge, Mark Crossley, Frans Hoek, Dino Zoff, Tony Godden, Alan Knight, Bryan Gunn, Phil Parkes, Pat Jennings, Alvin Martin, Dan Bentley, Sebastian Frey, Shaka Hislop, Joe Corrigan, Martyn Margetson, Paul Trevillion, Stuart Pearce, Alan Fettis, Tony Coton, Alan Miller, Hans Van Breukelen, Adam Sells, Peter Hucker, Mark Wallington, Andy Jacobs, David Seaman, Craig Forrest, Peter Wall, Frank Weigl... and all the Kids in Gloves and with their Heroes. Also thanks to David Herrmann-Meng, author of 'Rudi Hiden - Die Hand des Wunderteams',

for his help; Arthur Renard & Matteo Palmigiano for arranging the interview with Dino Zoff; and to Kai Wenzel for his help with the Toni Schumacher piece.

'Glove Story 2' was produced in partnership with Just Keepers. With thanks to Ian Milne and the team at JustKeepers.com.

Author royalties will be donated to Willow, the only UK charity supporting seriously ill 16 to 40 year olds through Special Days. This donation represents the collective effort of the whole team across these two pages. Find out more about Willow's work at willowfoundation.org.uk.

TEAMWORK

Grateful thanks to everyone who bought the *Glove Story 2* subscribers' package in advance.

Alan Walker-Harris | Jerry Boekel | Graeme Miller | Francesco Ressa
Marc Smith | Philip Dewell | Ross Morecroft | Wayne Roberts
Colm Furey | Siôn Blew | Jeff Sutherland | Paul Owens | Jack White
Matthew Williams | Steve Stacy | Neil Keepin | Scott Howard
Andy Dove | Evert Vorster | Dom Rickard | Greg Phillips | Gary Floate
Alan Thompsett - Reigate Town Reserves | Vincenzo Portelli
Barry Bell | Chris Cleverley | Joseph Pierce | Dominic Moore
John Rogers | Dominik Robbins | Leigh Hale | Brandon Bisnette
Andrew Taylor | Sam Pavlik | Goalkeeper Sharing | Manfred Tschenett
Adam Cordery | Andrew Sparkes | George Banks | Paul Stevenson
Andrew Humphries | Tom Balch | Neal Heard | Martin Jarvis
John Pietralski | Ben Lewens | Gavin Haigh | Russell Corin | Zack Page
Darren Ashton | Matthew Fox | Glyn Marshall | Mark Thornley
James Dee | David Fleming | Steve Lawton | Grant Richardson
Jon Redpath | Rob Richards | Mick Richards | Jason Quek
Stuart Hancocks | Kevin Connolly | Mike Thomas | Stephen Powell
Michael Morgan | Dave Phillips | Mark Allen | Duncan Lewis
Diane Woodrow | Craig Matthews | David Sheridan | Paul Woollam
Graham Weaver | Darren Wheater Lowe | Stephen Seymour
David McKegney | Garry Maloney | Paul Condon | Johnathan Rudland
Alexander Connon | Ron Rushing | Wayne Bullock | Simon Bourne
Stephen Taylor | Steven Mulholland | Neil Smithard | Jamie Stephens
Douglas Broman | Phil Moody | Peris Hatton | Mark Newman
Joe Hendron | John Fyfe | Anthony Cox | Richard Eden | Kevin Fewell
Kevin Mulvaney | Thomas Nicholls | Lee Harrison | Steve Crust
Andrew Blackman | Gary Stinson | Stephen Collins | Derek Reid
Neil MacLeod | Simon Barnard | Tony Maddox | Darren Healy

Wayne Tomlinson | Trevor King | Lee Roberts | Richard Preston
Stephen Brown | Matt Brown | Nathan Bennett | Justin Pannell
Stuart Ford - F-Line | Max Crowe | Vivion O'Connor | Dave Smith
Paul Reynolds | Patrick Smith | Jochen Koerner | Matthew Pickerill
Mark Taylor | James Stack | Matthew Freeman | Tom Kelly | Neil Shorter
William Beesley | Dave De Man Lapidoth | Dave Holmes | Rod Repton
Roger Watling | Paul Bettinson | Bob Bettinson | Martin Willcocks
Jamie Boyle | James Mitchell | Northstandcritic | Ian Jackson
Andrew Kimber | Eddie Kehoe | Philip Lowe | Callum Griffin
Matthew Lumb | Paul Clarkson | Ralf Meier-Pruemm | Larry O'Connor
Elvis DeMarchi | Jason Rockett | Craig Fletcher | Adam Thomas-Scarrott
Dave Clayton | Stuart Reilly | Shane Farrell | Stephen J Halliwell
Bradley Pike - Grassroots Goalies | Andrew Blackman | Simon Warren
Kevin Slabber | Danny Dixon | Lloyd Griffith | Russell Harper
Cesar Chavez | Mark Sambridge | Craig Anstey | Simon Ogburn
Jason Ellis | Ashley Markham | Robert Cowap | Matt Howarth
Sebastian Selke | Tracey Markham | Paul Thomas | Chris Grant
Danny Knight | Tony Maddox | Gary Hegarty | David Lucas
Anthony Krumhorn - KEEPERsport France | Sam Dickens | Adam Ding
Christian Davis | Adam Booth | Paul Orchard - In Off the Far Post
Paul Davie | Jason Lee | Alan Knight | David Coles | John Keeley
Paul Barton | Richard Murphy | Paul Bridson | James Dee
Richard Johnson | Darren Barnes | Luke Wheeler | Callum Finnie
John Williams | Ernie Bradwell | John Stokes | Chris Lynn | Vince Cox
Pete Weller | Daryl Roberts | Tyrone Hoare | Mark Harvey | Adam Sells
Darren Male | Danny Jones | Adrian Madeley | Mark Cannell
Graham Marsden | Martin Knowles | John Bromley | Alan Tyrrell

"An ode to the goalkeeper – too often football's overlooked scapegoat. Not only can you reconnect with your carefree childhood, but you are different – and often the difference. Goalkeepers get a bad rap. They deserve to be celebrated more than they have been. A fun ode to goalkeepers, bringing together an array of stories from the world of goalkeeping." **– The i Paper**

"The book for all with a goalkeeper's-eye view of the game. Packed full of exclusive interviews with some goalkeeping greats. You can read about the great brands, games, cartoon characters, kits and just about every other aspect... but you don't have to have been one to enjoy this book."
– The League Mag

"When it says it's the no.1 book for every goalkeeper it means it. A glorious collection of memorabilia and images touching on everything you can think of regarding goalies. If you're a fan of 'Got, Not Got' you'll like this. In addition, all the author royalties from the book go to the Willow Foundation."
– talkSPORT Christmas Gift Guide

"Packed with an easily digestible mix of photos, memories, memorabilia and large chunks of subjectivity. Great stuff." **– Sports Book of the Month**